EAGLE® BRAND

Best-Loved Desserts

71 Treats for Year-Round Fun

Meredith® Books
Des Moines, Iowa

This seal assures you that every recipe in *Best-Loved Desserts* has been tested in the *Better Homes and Gardens®* Test Kitchen. This means that each recipe is practical and reliable and meets high standards of taste appeal.

© 1999 Meredith Corporation and Eagle Family Foods, Inc.
All Rights Reserved. Printed in the United States of America.
Printing Number and Year: 5 4 3 2 1   03 02 01 00 99
Library of Congress Catalog Card Number: 99-70254
ISBN: 0-696-21004-5
Canadian BN: 12348 2887 RT
EAGLE BRAND is a registered trademark of Eagle Family Foods, Inc.
Elsie and Borden trademarks used under license from BDH Two, Inc.
Produced by Meredith Integrated Marketing, 1716 Locust Street, Des Moines, IA 50309-3023.
Better Homes and Gardens® Test Kitchen Seal is a registered trademark of Meredith Corporation.

Credits

Produced by:

Meredith® Books and
Meredith® Integrated Marketing,
1716 Locust Street,
Des Moines, IA 50309-3023.

Meredith® Books

Editor: Chuck Smothermon

Design Production: Craig Hanken

Proofreader: Susie Kling

Production Director:
Douglas M. Johnston

Editor in Chief: James D. Blume

Design Director: Matt Strelecki

Managing Editor: Gregory H. Kayko

Director, Sales & Marketing, Retail:
Michael A. Peterson

Director, Sales & Marketing,
Special Markets: Rita McMullen

Director, Operations: George A. Susral

Vice President, General Manager:
Jamie L. Martin

Above: *Marbled Cheesecake Hearts (see recipe, page 23)*
On front cover: *Welcome Home Chocolate Bars (see recipe, page 89), Chocolate Fantasy Bars (see recipe, page 22) and Foolproof Fudge with variations (see recipe, page 13)*

Welcome to Best-Loved Desserts

Eagle® Brand believes delicious, irresistible desserts are part of what makes life more enjoyable! We've designed our recipes to fit into your busy schedules, to be easy and foolproof so you don't have to desert dessert!

With the help of Eagle® Brand Sweetened Condensed Milk, the "magic ingredient" that has been a trusted, key element of baking and dessert-making for more than 142 years, you'll be pleasantly surprised at how easy it is to make time for these homemade treats.

Our dessert collection is full of new ideas as well as time-honored favorites that you will have fun making and sharing with family and loved ones. You'll find just the right treat or dessert for all life's moments—whether it's Valentine's Day, Easter Sunday, a picnic, a birthday party or simply a quiet evening at home. When you make an Eagle® Brand treat, you know it will turn out perfect every time.

So, take some time to savor the sweet life— the Eagle® Brand way.

*For more ways to **Make Magic In Minutes!**, visit us at*

www.eaglebrand.com

see page 4

see page 33

see page 70

EAGLE BRAND
Best-Loved
Desserts

Call us with questions and comments at
1-888-656-3245
Monday–Friday, 8 a.m. to 5:30 p.m. Eastern time

EAGLE BRAND

Best-Loved
Classics

Remember the "magic" of Seven Layer Magic Cookie Bars and the refreshing, tart-and-tingly Lemon Crumb Bars that showed up (if you were lucky) at the annual family picnic? Or, does your mouth water at the mention of rich, spicy Pumpkin Pride Pie that is an essential part of family Thanksgivings? This chapter has those recipes and other classic desserts that generations have come to know, love and anticipate.

Seven Layer Magic Cookie Bars (see recipe, page 6),
Lemon Crumb Bars (see recipe, page 6) and Pumpkin Pride Pie with new variations
(see recipe, page 7)

Seven Layer Magic Cookie Bars

They may have seven layers, but it's as easy as 1-2-3 to make these classic treats. Kids of all sizes will enjoy these "magic" bars (shown on pages 4–5).

Prep Time: 10 minutes   Baking Time: 25 minutes   Makes 24 to 36 bars

½ cup (1 stick) butter
     or margarine
1½ cups graham cracker crumbs
1 (14-ounce) can Eagle® Brand Sweetened Condensed Milk (NOT evaporated milk)
1 cup (6 ounces) butterscotch flavored chips*
1 cup (6 ounces) semi-sweet chocolate chips
1⅓ cups flaked coconut
1 cup chopped nuts

❶ Preheat oven to 350° (325° for glass dish). In 13x9-inch baking pan, melt butter in oven.

❷ Sprinkle crumbs over butter; pour Eagle Brand evenly over crumbs. Top with remaining ingredients; press down firmly with fork.

❸ Bake 25 minutes or until lightly browned. Cool. Chill if desired. Cut into bars. Store covered at room temperature.

*NOTE: Substitute peanut butter flavored chips or white chocolate chips for the butterscotch chips.

Lemon Crumb Bars

These unique lemony bars add refreshing flavor and variety to your cookie collection. Serve them at an afternoon tea or a picnic (shown on pages 4–5).

Prep Time: 10 minutes   Baking Time: 15 to 20 minutes + 25 minutes
Makes 24 to 36 bars

1 (18¼-ounce) package lemon *or* yellow cake mix
½ cup (1 stick) butter, softened
1 egg plus 3 egg yolks
2 cups finely crushed saltine crackers (4 ounces)
1 (14-ounce) can Eagle® Brand Sweetened Condensed Milk (NOT evaporated milk)
½ cup ReaLemon® Lemon Juice from Concentrate

❶ Preheat oven to 350°. With mixer, beat cake mix, butter and 1 egg in large bowl until crumbly. Stir in saltine crumbs. Set aside 2 cups crumb mixture. Press remaining crumb mixture on bottom of greased 13x9-inch baking pan. Bake 15 to 20 minutes or until golden.

❷ With mixer or wire whisk, beat 3 egg yolks with Eagle Brand and ReaLemon. Spread over prepared crust. Top with reserved crumb mixture. Bake 25 minutes longer or until set and top is golden. Cool. Refrigerate within 2 hours. Cut into bars. Store leftovers covered in refrigerator.

Pumpkin Pride Pie

It wouldn't be Thanksgiving without this sweetly spiced pie. Leave it unadorned, or try a chocolate, sour cream or streusel topping (shown on pages 4–5).

Prep Time: 20 minutes   Baking Time: 15 minutes + 35 to 40 minutes
Makes 6 to 8 servings

1   (15-ounce) can pumpkin
      (2 cups)
1   (14-ounce) can Eagle® Brand
      Sweetened Condensed Milk
      (NOT evaporated milk)
2   eggs
1   teaspoon ground cinnamon
½   teaspoon each: ground
      ginger, nutmeg *and* salt
1   (9-inch) unbaked pie crust
      (see tip, page 68)
      Chocolate Glaze, optional
      (recipe follows)

❶ Preheat oven to 425°. With mixer, beat pumpkin, Eagle Brand, eggs, spices and salt. Pour into crust. Bake 15 minutes. Reduce oven temperature to 350°; bake 35 to 40 minutes longer. Cool. Drizzle with Chocolate Glaze if desired. Refrigerate within 2 hours. Store leftovers covered in refrigerator.

PUMPKIN PIE TOPPING OPTIONS

Chocolate Glaze: In small saucepan, melt ½ cup semi-sweet chocolate chips with 1 teaspoon solid shortening.

Sour Cream Topping: Assemble pie as directed at left. Combine 1½ cups sour cream, 2 tablespoons sugar and 1 teaspoon vanilla extract. After pie has baked 30 minutes at 350°, spread mixture evenly over pie; bake 10 minutes longer.

Streusel Topping: Assemble pie as directed at left. Combine ½ cup packed light brown sugar and ½ cup unsifted flour; cut in ¼ cup cold butter until crumbly. Stir in ¼ cup chopped nuts. After pie has baked 30 minutes at 350°, sprinkle mixture on top of pie; bake 10 minutes longer.

Quick desserts are nothing new! Eagle® Brand has been offering easy, foolproof recipes since the 1920s.

Classics

Cherry-Topped Lemon Cheesecake Pie

This creamy no-bake pie takes only minutes to make. Stir it together in the morning for a company-special dessert that night.

Prep Time: 10 minutes   Chilling Time: 3 hours   Makes 6 to 8 servings

1 (8-ounce) package cream cheese, softened
1 (14-ounce) can Eagle® Brand Sweetened Condensed Milk (NOT evaporated milk)
⅓ cup ReaLemon® Lemon Juice from Concentrate
1 teaspoon vanilla extract
1 (6-ounce) purchased graham cracker crumb pie crust*
1 (21-ounce) can cherry pie filling, chilled

❶ With mixer, beat cream cheese in large bowl until fluffy. Gradually beat in Eagle Brand until smooth. Stir in ReaLemon and vanilla. Pour into crust. Chill at least 3 hours.

❷ To serve, top pie with cherry pie filling. Store leftovers covered in refrigerator.

*NOTE: For a firmer crust, brush crust with slightly beaten egg white; bake in 375° oven for 5 minutes. Cool; pour filling into crust. Chill.

Creamy Delight Cheesecake

A versatile classic, this velvety cheesecake is always in season. Serve it plain or give its creamy richness a fruity accent by spooning some of the ruby red raspberry sauce over each serving.

Prep Time: 20 minutes   Baking Time: 50 to 55 minutes
Cooling Time: 1 hour   Chilling Time: 4 hours   Makes 10 to 12 servings

1¼ cups graham cracker crumbs
⅓ cup butter *or* margarine, melted
¼ cup sugar
2 (8-ounce) packages cream cheese, softened
1 (14-ounce) can Eagle® Brand Sweetened Condensed Milk
   (NOT evaporated milk)
3 eggs
¼ cup ReaLemon® Lemon Juice from Concentrate
1 (8-ounce) container sour cream, at room temperature
   Raspberry Sauce, optional (recipe below)

❶ Preheat oven to 300°. Combine crumbs, butter and sugar; press firmly on bottom of 9-inch springform pan.

❷ With mixer, beat cream cheese in large bowl until fluffy. Gradually beat in Eagle Brand until smooth. Add eggs and ReaLemon; mix well.

❸ Pour into prepared pan. Bake 50 to 55 minutes or until center is set; top with sour cream. Bake 5 minutes longer. Cool 1 hour. Chill at least 4 hours.

❹ Serve with Raspberry Sauce if desired. Store leftovers covered in refrigerator.

TOPPING OPTION

Raspberry Sauce: In small saucepan, combine ⅔ cup syrup drained from 1 (10-ounce) package thawed frozen red raspberries, ¼ cup red currant jelly *or* red raspberry jam and 1 tablespoon cornstarch. Cook and stir until slightly thickened and clear. Cool. Stir in raspberries.

VARIATION

New York Style Cheesecake: Omit sour cream. Increase cream cheese to 4 (8-ounce) packages and eggs to 4. Add 2 tablespoons unsifted flour after eggs. Proceed as above. Bake 1 hour and 10 minutes or until center is set. Cool 1 hour. Chill at least 4 hours. Serve with Raspberry Sauce if desired. Store as above.

magic ingredient

Classics

Fresh Fruit Ice Cream

Eagle® Brand makes the easiest ice cream ever! Cool down with this homemade ice cream that is sure to be a highlight at any get-together. Make it with one fruit or a combination of your favorites.

Prep Time: 10 minutes   Freezing Time: 40 minutes
Makes about 1½ quarts (10 to 12 servings)

- 3 cups (1½ pints) half-and-half *or* light cream
- 1 (14-ounce) can Eagle® Brand Sweetened Condensed Milk (NOT evaporated milk)
- 1 cup mashed *or* pureed fresh fruit, such as peaches, strawberries, bananas *and/or* raspberries
- 1 tablespoon vanilla extract
-    Several drops food coloring, optional

❶ In 2-quart ice cream freezer container, combine all ingredients; mix well.

❷ Freeze according to manufacturer's instructions. Store leftovers in freezer.

VARIATIONS

Vanilla Ice Cream: Omit fruit and food coloring. Increase half-and-half *or* light cream to 4 cups. Proceed as directed.

Refrigerator-Freezer Method: Omit half-and-half. In large bowl, combine Eagle Brand and vanilla; stir in 1 cup pureed fruit and food coloring if desired. Fold in 2 cups (1 pint) whipping cream, whipped to soft peaks (do not use non-dairy whipped topping). Pour into 9x5-inch loaf pan or a 2-quart freezer container; cover. Freeze 6 hours or until firm.

Eagle® Brand *tip*

Foolproof Ice Cream

Homemade ice cream is easy to make when you use Eagle® Brand Sweetened Condensed Milk. Eagle® Brand blends easily with other ingredients and lends rich, thick consistency so eggs are not needed. The low freezing point of Eagle® Brand helps minimize the formation of ice crystals so the ice cream turns out smooth and creamy every time.

Fresh Fruit Ice Cream (see recipe above)
and Key Lime Pie (see recipe, page 12)

Key Lime Pie

There's a bit of sunshine in every creamy bite of this classic meringue-topped pie (shown on page 11). Its cool taste is perfect with a cup of coffee.

Prep Time: 25 minutes   Baking Time: 30 minutes + 15 minutes
Cooling Time: 1 hour   Chilling Time: 3 hours   Makes 8 servings

- 3 eggs, separated
- 1 (14-ounce) can Eagle® Brand Sweetened Condensed Milk (NOT evaporated milk)
- ½ cup ReaLime® Lime Juice from Concentrate
- 2 *or* 3 drops green food coloring, optional
- 1 (9-inch) unbaked pie crust (see tip, page 68)
- ½ teaspoon cream of tartar
- ⅓ cup sugar

❶ Preheat oven to 325°. With mixer, beat egg yolks in medium-sized bowl; gradually beat in Eagle Brand and ReaLime. Stir in food coloring if desired. Pour into pie crust.

❷ Bake 30 minutes. Remove from oven. Increase oven temperature to 350°.

❸ Meanwhile, for meringue, with clean mixer, beat egg whites with cream of tartar to soft peaks. Gradually beat in sugar, 1 tablespoon at a time; beat 4 minutes longer or until stiff, glossy peaks form and sugar is dissolved.

❹ Immediately spread meringue over hot pie, carefully sealing to edge of crust to prevent meringue from shrinking. Bake 15 minutes. Cool 1 hour. Chill at least 3 hours. Store leftovers covered in refrigerator.

Eagle® Brand, first introduced in 1856, has changed packages through the years, but the rich, creamy taste that won the hearts of consumers has stayed the same.

Foolproof Fudge

Great for holidays, birthdays and just right for giving away, this rich, creamy, no-fail fudge can be adorned with nuts, peanut butter chips or miniature marshmallows (shown on the cover).

Prep Time: 10 minutes   Chilling Time: 2 hours   Makes about 2 pounds

3 cups (18 ounces) semi-sweet chocolate chips
1 (14-ounce) can Eagle® Brand Original *or* Creamy Chocolate Sweetened Condensed Milk (NOT evaporated milk)
   Dash salt
½ to 1 cup chopped nuts, optional
1½ teaspoons vanilla extract

❶ Line 8- or 9-inch square pan with foil. Butter foil; set aside.

❷ In heavy saucepan, melt chips with Eagle Brand and salt. Remove from heat; stir in nuts if desired and the vanilla. Spread evenly into prepared pan.

❸ Chill 2 hours or until firm. Turn fudge onto cutting board; peel off foil and cut into squares. Store covered in refrigerator.

VARIATIONS

Peanut Butter Chip Glazed Fudge: Omit nuts. Stir ¾ cup peanut butter flavored chips in with vanilla. Spread in pan and chill as above. For glaze, in small saucepan, melt ½ cup peanut butter flavored chips with ½ cup whipping cream; stir until thick and smooth. Spread over chilled fudge. Chill. Cut and store as directed above.

Marshmallow Fudge: Omit nuts. Stir 2 tablespoons butter in with vanilla. Fold in 2 cups miniature marshmallows. Proceed as above.

Eagle® Brand *tip*

Creative Cuts

For perfectly cut candies or bar cookies (and easy clean up), try this tip:
• Line the entire pan, including the sides, with aluminum foil before adding the cookie batter or candy mixture.
• When cool, lift the edges of the foil to remove the block from the pan.
• Cut the block into squares, rectangles or diamonds.
• To make diamonds, cut straight lines 1 to 1½ inches apart down length of the block. Then, diagonally cut straight lines 1 to 1½ inches apart across block.

Coconut Macaroons

These bite-size cookies are toasty on the outside, moist on the inside and chock-full of chewy coconut.

Prep Time: 10 minutes   Baking Time: 15 to 17 minutes
Makes about 4 dozen

- 1 (14-ounce) can Eagle® Brand Sweetened Condensed Milk (NOT evaporated milk)
- 2 teaspoons vanilla extract
- 1 to 1½ teaspoons almond extract
- 2 (7-ounce) packages flaked coconut (5⅓ cups)

❶ Preheat oven to 325°. Line baking sheets with foil; grease and flour foil. Set aside.

❷ In large bowl, combine Eagle Brand, vanilla and almond extract.

Stir in coconut. Drop by rounded teaspoonfuls onto foil-lined sheets; with spoon, slightly flatten each mound.

❸ Bake 15 to 17 minutes or until golden. Remove from baking sheets; cool on wire rack. Store loosely covered at room temperature.

VARIATION

Macaroon Kisses: Prepare and bake as above. Press solid milk chocolate candy star *or* drop in center of each macaroon immediately after baking.

Creamy Caramel Flans

One bite of this silky, custardy dessert of Spanish origin will make you a lifelong fan of flan (pronounced "flahn").

Prep Time: 15 minutes   Baking Time: 30 to 35 minutes
Chilling Time: 2 hours   Makes 8 servings

¾ cup sugar
4 eggs
1¾ cups water
1 (14-ounce) can Eagle® Brand Sweetened Condensed Milk (NOT evaporated milk)
1 teaspoon vanilla extract
⅛ teaspoon salt
    Sugar Garnish, optional (recipe follows)

❶ Preheat oven to 350°. In heavy skillet, over medium heat, cook and stir sugar until melted and caramel-colored. Pour into 8 ungreased 6-ounce custard cups, tilting to coat bottoms.

❷ With mixer or wire whisk, beat eggs in large bowl; stir in water, Eagle Brand, vanilla and salt. Pour into prepared custard cups. Set cups in large shallow pan. Fill pan with 1 inch hot water.

❸ Bake 30 to 35 minutes or until knife inserted near centers comes out clean. Cool. Chill at least 2 hours. To serve, invert flans onto individual serving plates. Top with Sugar Garnish or garnish as desired. Store leftovers covered in refrigerator.

Sugar Garnish: Fill a medium-sized metal bowl half-full of ice. In medium-sized saucepan, combine 1 cup sugar with ¼ cup water. Stir; cover and bring to a boil. Cook over high heat 5 to 6 minutes or until light brown in color. Immediately put pan in ice for 1 minute. Using spoon, carefully drizzle sugar decoratively over foil. Cool. To serve, peel from foil.

**Shortcut Eagle®
Brand recipes earned
the name "magic
recipes" in the 1940s.**

© The Borden Company 1942 and 1940

Classics

Mocha Tiramisu

Once trendy, this chocolate-and-coffee-flavored Italian dessert (whose name translates literally as "pick me up") is now firmly entrenched as a classic.

Prep Time: 30 minutes   Chilling Time: 4 hours   Makes 8 servings

2   tablespoons instant
      coffee crystals
½   cup hot water
2   (3-ounce) packages
      ladyfingers (24), cut
      crosswise into quarters
1   (14-ounce) can Eagle® Brand
      Sweetened Condensed Milk
      (NOT evaporated milk)
8   ounces mascarpone *or*
      cream cheese, softened
2   cups (1 pint) whipping cream
1   teaspoon vanilla extract
1   cup (6 ounces) miniature
      semi-sweet chocolate
      chips
      Grated semi-sweet
      chocolate *and/or*
      strawberries, optional

❶ Dissolve coffee crystals in hot water; set aside 1 tablespoon of the coffee mixture. Brush remaining coffee mixture on cut sides of ladyfingers; set aside.

❷ With mixer, gradually beat ¾ cup of the Eagle Brand into mascarpone in large bowl. Add 1¼ cups of the whipping cream, vanilla and reserved coffee mixture; beat until soft peaks form. Fold in half of the chips.

❸ In small saucepan, melt remaining chips with remaining Eagle Brand. Using 8 tall dessert glasses or parfait glasses, layer mascarpone mixture, chocolate mixture and ladyfinger pieces, beginning and ending with mascarpone mixture. Cover and chill at least 4 hours.

❹ To serve, with mixer, beat remaining whipping cream until soft peaks form. Spoon whipped cream over layered desserts. Garnish with grated chocolate and strawberries if desired. Store leftovers covered in refrigerator.

Eagle® Brand *tip*

Melting Chocolate

Chocolate melts smoothly with Eagle® Brand. For a velvety texture, be sure to use a medium to heavy saucepan and low heat. As the chocolate heats, stir the mixture constantly until it is smooth. If the heat is too high, the chocolate may form tiny clumps.

Classics

Cappuccino Frost

Whether you make it plain or with almond or mint, you're sure to enjoy this refreshing coffeehouse favorite (shown in tall mug, opposite page).

Prep Time: 5 minutes   Makes 5 servings

1 (14-ounce) can Eagle® Brand Original *or* Creamy Chocolate Sweetened Condensed Milk (NOT evaporated milk)
2 cups cold water
1 tablespoon instant coffee crystals
1 cup ice cubes

❶ In blender container, combine Eagle Brand, water and coffee crystals. Add ice cubes. Cover and blend until smooth and frothy.

VARIATIONS

Almond Cappuccino Frost: Add 2 tablespoons amaretto *or* crème d'amande *or* ¼ teaspoon almond extract. Proceed as directed above.

Minty Cappuccino Frost: Add 2 tablespoons crème de mint *or* ¼ teaspoon mint extract. Proceed as directed above.

Cranberry-Apple Punch

Serve this foamy, fruit-flavored drink for any occasion. It's especially refreshing during the summer heat (shown in short mug, opposite page).

Prep Time: 10 minutes   Makes about 25 servings

1 (14-ounce) can Eagle® Brand Sweetened Condensed Milk (NOT evaporated milk), chilled
1 (12-ounce) can frozen cranberry-apple juice concentrate *or* other frozen apple juice concentrate blends, thawed
⅓ cup ReaLemon® Lemon Juice from Concentrate
1 (1-liter) bottle carbonated water, chilled
 Ice cubes
 Fresh cranberries, optional

❶ In large punch bowl, combine Eagle Brand, juice concentrate and ReaLemon.

❷ Gently stir in carbonated water. Serve at once over ice. Garnish with cranberries if desired.

TIP: Tint punch a brighter pink with a few drops red food coloring if desired.

From back: Cappuccino Frost and Cranberry-Apple Punch (see recipes above)

Year-Round
Dessert Ideas
Made Special

From January to December, special events call for special desserts. If you've got a dessert-worthy celebration coming up (and who doesn't?), you'll find the perfect recipe on the following pages. Whether you choose Peppermint Easter Eggs for Easter, Chocolate Ice Cream Cake for a birthday party or Strawberry Splash Punch for a New Year's Eve party, the desserts in this chapter will make your celebration extra special.

Chocolate Ice Cream Cake (see recipe, page 29), Peppermint Easter Eggs (see recipe, page 25) and Strawberry Splash Punch (see recipe, page 41)

Chocolate Fantasy Bars

Start the year off by scoring big with these double-chocolate bars at your Super Bowl party (shown on cover). And, for a refreshing halftime break, pair the bars with Fruit Smoothies (see recipe, page 46).

Prep Time: 15 minutes   Baking Time: 25 to 30 minutes   Makes 24 to 36 bars

1   (18¼- *or* 18½-ounce) package chocolate cake mix
⅓   cup vegetable oil
1   egg
1   cup chopped nuts
1   cup (6 ounces) semi-sweet chocolate chips
1   (14-ounce) can Eagle® Brand Original *or* Creamy Chocolate Sweetened Condensed Milk (NOT evaporated milk)
1   teaspoon vanilla extract
    Dash salt
    Purchased tube of decorating icing, optional

❶ Preheat oven to 350°. With mixer on medium speed, beat cake mix, oil and egg in large bowl until crumbly. Stir in nuts. Set aside 1 cup of the crumb mixture. Firmly press remaining crumb mixture on bottom of greased 13x9-inch baking pan.

❷ In small saucepan, melt chips with Eagle Brand, vanilla and salt. Pour evenly over prepared crust. Sprinkle reserved crumb mixture evenly over top. Bake 25 to 30 minutes or until edges are firm. Cool. Cut into bars. Drizzle with icing if desired. Store loosely covered at room temperature.

Decorating Idea: For a special Super Bowl touch, use icing to write team names and draw footballs on the bars. Then, watch the competition eat them up.

Eagle® Brand is the dessert/treat maker that cooks have counted on for success for over 142 years.

1998

1946

Marbled Cheesecake Hearts

These luscious heart-shaped bars will win your Valentine's heart any day of the year (shown on page 2).

Prep Time: 20 minutes   Baking Time: 45 to 50 minutes
Chilling Time: 1 hour   Makes about 12 (3-inch) hearts

2   cups finely crushed creme-filled chocolate sandwich cookies (about 24 cookies)
3   tablespoons butter *or* margarine, melted
3   (8-ounce) packages cream cheese, softened
1   (14-ounce) can Eagle® Brand Sweetened Condensed Milk (NOT evaporated milk)
3   eggs
2   teaspoons vanilla extract
2   (1-ounce) squares unsweetened chocolate, melted

❶ Preheat oven to 300°. Line a 13x9-inch baking pan with heavy foil; set aside.

❷ Combine crumbs and butter; press firmly on bottom of foil-lined pan.

❸ With mixer, beat cream cheese in large bowl until fluffy. Gradually beat in Eagle Brand until smooth. Add eggs and vanilla; mix well. Pour half the batter evenly over prepared crust.

❹ Stir melted chocolate into remaining batter; spoon over vanilla batter. With table knife or metal spatula, gently swirl chocolate batter through vanilla batter to marble.

❺ Bake 45 to 50 minutes or until set. Cool. Chill at least 1 hour. Use foil to lift out of pan. For hearts, cut with heart-shaped cookie cutter or, with knife, cut around waxed paper heart shape. Or, cut into bars. Store leftovers covered in refrigerator.

Eagle® Brand *tip*

Chocolate-Dipped Fruit

Cap off any celebration with an impressive, yet quick, dessert. Simply pour Eagle® Brand Creamy Chocolate Sweetened Condensed Milk into a pretty glass bowl. Then, serve it with whole strawberries and apple, pear or banana slices.

Lucky Mint Cheesecake

Give this yummy mint-and-chocolate cheesecake a St. Patrick's Day touch by piping melted chocolate into a shamrock shape on each piece.

Prep Time: 15 minutes   Baking Time: 25 minutes
Chilling Time: 3 hours   Makes 8 servings

½ cup (3 ounces) semi-sweet chocolate chips
1 (14-ounce) can Eagle® Brand Sweetened Condensed Milk (NOT evaporated milk)
1 teaspoon vanilla extract
1 (6-ounce) purchased chocolate flavored crumb pie crust
11 ounces cream cheese,* softened
½ teaspoon mint extract
   Several drops green food coloring
1 egg

❶ Preheat oven to 350°. In small saucepan, melt chips with ⅓ cup of the Eagle Brand. Stir in vanilla. Spread on bottom of pie crust.

❷ With mixer, beat cream cheese in large bowl until fluffy; gradually beat in remaining Eagle Brand, mint extract and green food coloring. Add egg; beat on low speed just until combined. Place pie crust on baking sheet; place on oven rack. Carefully pour mint mixture over chocolate layer in pie crust.

❸ Bake 25 minutes or until center is nearly set. Cool. Chill at least 3 hours. Store leftovers covered in refrigerator.

*NOTE: Use 1 (8-ounce) package plus 1 (3-ounce) package cream cheese.

Peppermint Easter Eggs

Kids of all ages will be delighted to find these colorfully decorated, creamy candy eggs in the basket left by the Easter Bunny (shown on pages 20–21).

Prep Time: 50 minutes plus decorating   Chilling Time: 4 hours
Makes 40 eggs

½ cup butter, softened
½ teaspoon salt
1 (14-ounce) can Eagle® Brand Sweetened Condensed Milk (NOT evaporated milk)
½ teaspoon peppermint extract
2 drops red food coloring
9 to 10 cups sifted powdered sugar
½ cup crushed peppermint candies (about 20 candies)
1 (24-ounce) package vanilla flavored candy coating *or* confectioners' coating
Purchased tubes of decorating icings

❶ With mixer, beat butter and salt in large bowl. Gradually beat in Eagle Brand, peppermint extract and food coloring. Gradually beat in 6 cups of the powdered sugar. With spoon, stir in as much of the remaining powdered sugar as you can. Stir in crushed candies.

❷ Turn onto surface dusted with additional powdered sugar.

Gradually knead in enough of the remaining powdered sugar to make a smooth, easy-to-shape mixture. Divide into quarters. Shape each quarter into 10 eggs (each about 2 inches long and 1 to 1½ inches wide). Place eggs on waxed-paper-lined baking sheets; cover and chill 4 hours or until firm.

❸ In large saucepan, melt candy coating over low heat, stirring constantly. To coat each egg, insert fork into bottom of chilled egg and dip into warm candy coating; let excess coating drip off. Place on waxed-paper-lined baking sheets; let stand until firm. Decorate as desired with purchased icings. Store covered at room temperature or in refrigerator.

VARIATION

Peanut Butter Eggs: Reduce butter to ¼ cup; add ⅓ cup creamy peanut butter. Omit salt, peppermint extract, red food coloring and peppermint candies. Proceed as above.

In 1856, Gail Borden created Eagle® Brand as a reliable source of milk for infants, but cooks soon learned what a terrific ingredient it makes for baking.

Lime-Filled Pastry with Mixed Berries

A perfect-as-a-dream bridal shower is easy yet elegant when you serve this pretty, lime cream-filled puff pastry dessert with Cranberry-Apple Punch (see recipe, page 18) and tea.

Prep Time: 35 minutes   Baking Time: 20 to 25 minutes
Chilling Time: Up to 4 hours   Makes 8 to 10 servings

- 1 sheet frozen puff pastry (one-half 17¼-ounce package)
- 1 egg white, slightly beaten
  Coarse sugar *or* granulated sugar
- 1 (14-ounce) can Eagle® Brand Sweetened Condensed Milk (NOT evaporated milk)
- ⅓ cup ReaLime® Lime Juice from Concentrate
- ⅓ cup sour cream
- 3 cups fresh raspberries, blueberries, blackberries *and/or* quartered strawberries

❶ Let folded pastry thaw at room temperature for 20 minutes. Preheat oven to 375°. On a lightly floured surface, unfold pastry; roll out into 15x10-inch rectangle. Cut a ¾-inch-wide strip from each long side of rectangle; cut a ¾-inch-wide strip from each short end of rectangle. Set aside the 4 strips.

❷ Place pastry rectangle on ungreased baking sheet. Brush with egg white. Lay pastry strips on top of pastry rectangle, aligning outer edges of strips with outer edges of rectangle; trim strips to fit. Brush strips with egg white and sprinkle with sugar. Prick bottom of rectangle several times with fork.

❸ Bake 20 to 25 minutes or until light brown. Cool.

❹ In medium-sized bowl, combine Eagle Brand, ReaLime and sour cream. Spoon into cooled pastry rectangle. Cover and chill for up to 4 hours. Top with berries before serving. Store leftovers covered in refrigerator.

Eagle® Brand *tip*

Recipe for Success

Beginners and experienced cooks love cooking with Eagle® Brand Sweetened Condensed Milk because it guarantees success and gives confidence when making desserts. It thickens almost magically without cooking when mixed with lemon, lime or orange juice (in the recipe above the filling thickens when ReaLime® is stirred into Eagle® Brand). This means no worries about runny pie filling or pudding when you use Eagle® Brand.

Lemon Angel Dessert

Just the thing for the kids and dad to make for mom on Mother's Day, this angel food cake holds a surprise inside: creamy lemon filling and a medley of summer berries.

Prep Time: 15 minutes   Chilling Time: 4 hours   Makes 10 servings

1   (8- to 9-inch) angel food cake
1   (14-ounce) can Eagle® Brand Fat Free Sweetened Condensed Milk (NOT evaporated milk)
½   cup ReaLemon® Lemon Juice from Concentrate
1½   cups fresh raspberries, blueberries, blackberries *and/or* chopped strawberries
     Sifted powdered sugar, optional
     Fresh raspberries, blueberries, blackberries *and/or* strawberries, optional

❶ With serrated knife, cut 2-inch-thick layer horizontally off top of cake; lift off top and set aside. With fork, carefully hollow out bottom of cake, leaving ½- to ¾-inch-thick shell on bottom and sides.

❷ In medium-sized bowl, stir together Eagle Brand and ReaLemon until thickened. Spoon into cake shell. Spoon 1½ cups berries over Eagle Brand mixture; replace cake top. Cover and chill at least 4 hours.

❸ Just before serving, sprinkle with powdered sugar. Garnish with additional berries if desired. Store leftovers in refrigerator.

TIP: Use a serrated knife to slice the filled cake.

Chocolate Ice Cream Cake

Make any birthday extra-special with this celebratory dessert that features a rich vanilla ice cream nestled between layers of chocolate cake (shown on pages 20–21).

Prep Time: 25 minutes   Chilling Time: 30 minutes
Freezing Time: 1½ hours + 6 hours   Makes 10 servings

- 2 cups (1 pint) whipping cream
- 1 (14-ounce) can Eagle® Brand Sweetened Condensed Milk (NOT evaporated milk)
- 1 tablespoon vanilla extract
- ¾ cup miniature semi-sweet chocolate chips, optional
- 2 (9-inch) baked chocolate cake layers
- 1 to 2 tablespoons milk
- 1 (16-ounce) can chocolate frosting
    Purchased tubes of decorating icings

❶ Line an 8-inch baking pan with plastic wrap; set aside.

❷ In large bowl, combine whipping cream, Eagle Brand and vanilla. Cover and chill 30 minutes. With mixer, beat 4 to 5 minutes or until soft peaks form. Cover and freeze 1½ hours or until partially frozen. Gently fold in chips if desired. Spoon into prepared pan. Cover and freeze at least 6 hours.

❸ When ice cream is firm, set 1 cake layer on serving platter. Invert ice cream onto cake layer; remove plastic wrap. Top with remaining cake. Stir enough of the milk into frosting to reach slightly soft spreading consistency. Quickly spread cake and ice cream with frosting. Loosely cover with plastic wrap; freeze until serving time.

❹ Remove from freezer 15 minutes before serving; decorate as desired with purchased icings. Store leftovers covered in freezer.

Eagle® Brand *tip*

Easy Treats

Eagle® Brand is a simply wonderful way to add a sweet touch to any day:

- Spread it on warm muffins or toast.
- Offer it as a topper for waffles and French toast.
- Pour it directly into a pretty bowl for a fruit dip.
- Spoon some over cake instead of frosting.
- Stir it into coffee or tea for a coffeehouse-type beverage.

Tropical Orange Pie

Celebrate summer with this cool and creamy, pineapple-and-orange pie that's just right for Memorial Day or casual get-togethers.

Prep Time: 15 minutes   Baking Time: 35 to 40 minutes   Cooling Time: 1 hour
Chilling Time: 3 hours   Makes 8 servings

1 (9-inch) unbaked pie crust (see tip, page 68)
3 eggs
1 (14-ounce) can Eagle® Brand Sweetened Condensed Milk (NOT evaporated milk)
¾ cup frozen pineapple-orange juice concentrate *or* orange juice concentrate, thawed
⅓ cup water
2 tablespoons ReaLemon® Lemon Juice from Concentrate
¾ cup whipping cream

❶ Preheat oven to 325°. Prick pie crust all over with fork. Bake 8 to 10 minutes or until set and dry.

❷ For filling, with rotary beater or fork, beat eggs in medium-sized bowl. Gradually stir in Eagle Brand. Stir in juice concentrate, water and ReaLemon.

❸ Spoon filling into partially baked pie crust. Bake 35 to 40 minutes or until set. Cool 1 hour.

❹ Cover and chill at least 3 hours. To serve, with mixer, beat whipping cream until soft peaks form. Spread over pie. Store leftovers covered in refrigerator.

Eagle® Brand *tip*

Playing It Safe

Warm weather and eating outdoors go hand-in-hand. To make sure the foods you serve at backyard barbecues or for dinners on the deck are safe, remember to keep hot foods hot and cold foods cold.

• Hot foods should stay above 140°.

• Cold foods are best chilled on a bed of ice. Don't allow any foods to stand out longer than 2 hours—even if the food looks just fine.

Triple Chocolate Cheesecakes

Treat dad on Father's Day—or any other day—with this chocolate delight that can be served either frozen or chilled.

Prep Time: 20 minutes   Chilling Time: 4 hours
Makes 2 cheesecakes (12 servings total)

1 envelope unflavored gelatin
½ cup cold water
1 (14-ounce) can Eagle® Brand Sweetened Condensed Milk (NOT evaporated milk)
2 (8-ounce) packages cream cheese, softened
4 (1-ounce) squares unsweetened chocolate, melted and slightly cooled
1 (8-ounce) carton frozen non-dairy whipped topping, thawed
½ cup (3 ounces) miniature semi-sweet chocolate chips
1 (21-ounce) can cherry pie filling, optional
2 (6-ounce) purchased chocolate flavored crumb pie crusts

❶ In 1-cup glass measure, stir together the gelatin and cold water; let stand 5 minutes to soften. Pour about 1 inch water into small saucepan; place measure in saucepan. Place saucepan over medium heat; stir until gelatin is dissolved. Remove measure from saucepan; cool slightly.

❷ In large bowl, combine Eagle Brand, cream cheese and melted chocolate. With mixer, beat until smooth. Gradually beat in gelatin mixture. Fold in whipped topping and chips.

❸ Spread pie filling on bottoms of pie crusts if desired. Spoon chocolate mixture into pie crusts. Cover and chill at least 4 hours. Store leftovers covered in refrigerator.

TIP: To store this cheesecake in the freezer, cover and freeze up to 1 month. Serve frozen, or remove from freezer several hours before serving and let thaw in the refrigerator.

treats for dad

Berry Patriotic Trifle

Happy Independence Day! This red, white and blueberry trifle is sure to stir patriotic feelings—not to mention cravings for something sweet to eat.

Prep Time: 30 minutes   Chilling Time: 2 hours   Makes 6 to 8 servings

1¾ cups fresh blueberries
1 (14-ounce) can Eagle® Brand Sweetened Condensed Milk (NOT evaporated milk)
1 tablespoon ReaLemon® Lemon Juice from Concentrate
1 (10¾-ounce) loaf frozen pound cake
1 (4-serving size) package instant lemon pudding mix
1½ cups milk
½ cup sour cream
1½ cups fresh raspberries
  Star Garnish (recipe follows), optional

❶ With fork, mash ¼ cup of the blueberries in small bowl. Stir in 2 tablespoons of the Eagle Brand and ReaLemon.

❷ Halve pound cake horizontally. Spread blueberry mixture on cut side of bottom of cake; add cake top. Cut lengthwise into 4 strips; cut crosswise into 1-inch-thick pieces.

❸ With mixer, beat remaining Eagle Brand, pudding mix and milk in large bowl. Fold in sour cream.

❹ Set aside ¼ cup of the pudding mixture. In 2- to 2½-quart clear glass bowl, layer half of the pound cake pieces, half of the remaining pudding, half of the remaining blueberries and half of the raspberries. Repeat layers. Spoon on reserved pudding mixture. Cover and chill at least 2 hours. Store leftovers covered in refrigerator.

Star Garnish: Place 1 (1-ounce) white baking bar in heavy small saucepan. Heat over low heat until melted, stirring constantly. Tint melted white baking bar with red paste food coloring. Pipe mixture into star shapes on waxed-paper-lined baking sheet. Let stand until dry. Carefully peel from waxed paper.

Make-Ahead Fruit Juice Slush

*When the temperatures rise, keep this refreshing fruit slush on hand in the
freezer, ready to serve drop-in guests.*

Prep Time: 10 minutes   Freezing Time: 6 hours   Makes 10 servings

- 2 cups fresh *or* thawed frozen strawberries
- 1 (14-ounce) can Eagle® Brand Sweetened Condensed Milk (NOT evaporated milk)
- 1 (6-ounce) can frozen lemonade concentrate, thawed
- 1 (6-ounce) can frozen pineapple juice concentrate, thawed
- 4 cups (1 quart) orange juice Carbonated water, chilled

❶ In blender container, combine strawberries, Eagle Brand, lemonade concentrate and pineapple juice concentrate; cover and blend until smooth. Pour into large bowl; stir in orange juice. Transfer to a large shallow freezer container. Freeze 6 hours or until firm.

❷ Remove from freezer 20 minutes before serving. To serve, scrape spoon across surface of frozen mixture; spoon into glasses to fill each half full. Fill glasses with carbonated water; stir gently.

Island Oasis Smoothies

*Toast summer at your next barbecue with this refreshing double-fruit shake.
Choose papaya, mango, kiwifruit or banana to pair with the pineapple.*

Prep Time: 10 minutes   Makes 6 servings

- 1 (14-ounce) can Eagle® Brand Sweetened Condensed Milk (NOT evaporated milk)
- 1 (8-ounce) can crushed pineapple packed with juice
- 1 (8-ounce) carton vanilla yogurt
- 1 medium papaya *or* mango, peeled, seeded and cut up, *or* 1 medium banana *or* 2 medium kiwi fruit, peeled and cut up
- 1½ cups ice cubes

❶ In blender container, combine Eagle Brand, pineapple with juice, yogurt and papaya; cover and blend until smooth.

❷ Add ice cubes; cover and blend until smooth. Serve immediately.

Peanut Butter Jammers

Guarantee a great first day back-to-school! Tuck these sweet bar cookies, similar to every student's favorite sandwich, into a sack lunch.

Prep Time: 25 minutes   Baking Time: 25 minutes   Makes 60 bars

1   (14-ounce) can Eagle® Brand
     Sweetened Condensed Milk
     (NOT evaporated milk)
½   cup peanut butter
1   cup (2 sticks) butter
2   cups packed brown sugar
1   teaspoon baking soda
2   eggs
2   teaspoons vanilla extract
2½ cups unsifted flour
3   cups rolled oats
½   cup jelly, any flavor

❶ Preheat oven to 350°. In medium-sized bowl, combine Eagle Brand and peanut butter; set aside.

❷ With mixer, beat butter in large bowl 30 seconds. Add brown sugar and baking soda; beat until combined. Beat in eggs and vanilla. Beat in as much of the flour as you can with the mixer. Stir in remaining flour and oats.

❸ Press two-thirds (about 3⅓ cups) of the oat mixture on bottom of ungreased 15x10-inch baking pan. Carefully spread peanut butter mixture over. Drop jelly in small dollops (¼ to ½ teaspoon each) evenly over peanut butter mixture. Dot with remaining oat mixture.

❹ Bake 25 minutes or until top is lightly browned. Cool. Cut into bars. Store covered at room temperature.

Eagle® Brand *tip*

Butter versus Margarine

Many of the recipes in this book call for butter to assure optimum flavor and texture. If you would like to use margarine in place of butter, make sure the margarine you use is at least 80 percent vegetable oil or fat. Any product with less than 80 percent vegetable oil or fat contains additional water and milk solids and can make your baked goods either soggy or rock hard.

Ghostly Good Caramel Apples

Caramel apples are a Halloween classic, but these chewy treats feature a twist on tradition: a costume of chocolate flavored crisp rice cereal.

Prep Time: 20 minutes   Cooking Time: 25 minutes   Makes 16 servings

16   small apples
        (about 4 pounds)
16   wooden sticks
  2   cups packed brown sugar
  1   (14-ounce) can Eagle® Brand
        Creamy Chocolate *or* Original
        Sweetened Condensed Milk
        (NOT evaporated milk)
  1   cup light corn syrup
  ½   cup (1 stick) butter
  1   teaspoon vanilla extract
  2   cups chocolate flavored
        crisp rice cereal

❶ Wash and dry apples. Remove stems. Insert a wooden stick into the stem end of each apple; set aside.

❷ In heavy 3-quart saucepan, combine brown sugar, Eagle Brand, corn syrup and butter. Bring to boil, stirring constantly. Boil gently over medium heat, stirring frequently, 25 minutes. Remove from heat; stir in vanilla.

❸ Line baking sheets with foil; grease foil. Working quickly, dip each apple into the hot caramel mixture; use a spoon if necessary to spread mixture evenly over apples. Allow excess mixture to drip off. Dip bottoms of apples into cereal. Place on greased foil; let stand until firm, about 25 minutes. Store uncovered at room temperature.

Eagle® Brand *tip*

Scare Up Some Fun

Halloween is a bewitching time for a party. Here's some of our favorite tricks:

• Let the kids help choose a theme for the party. Invite guests to come as their favorite animals, as clowns or as storybook characters.

• Select a few simple games, read spooky stories or ask the children to tell jokes or perform magic tricks for entertainment.

• For treats, choose a few easy recipes, such as Ghostly Good Caramel Apples (above) or Jolly Jack-O'-Lantern Tarts (see recipe, page 38).

Ghostly Good Caramel Apples (see recipe above) and Jolly Jack-O'-Lantern Tarts (see recipe, page 38)

Jolly Jack-O'-Lantern Tarts

Garner bowls of appreciation with these terrific tarts (shown on page 36).

Prep Time: 20 minutes plus decorating   Chilling Time: 1 hour   Makes 12 servings

1   (14-ounce) can Eagle® Brand Creamy Chocolate *or* Original Sweetened Condensed Milk (NOT evaporated milk)
1   tablespoon orange juice concentrate, thawed
1   (4-serving size) package instant chocolate pudding mix
4   ounces (one-half 8-ounce container) frozen non-dairy whipped topping, thawed
2   (4-ounce) packages single serve graham cracker pie crusts*
    Nonstick spray coating
    Orange colored sprinkles
6   green gumdrops, halved

❶ In large bowl, combine Eagle Brand and orange juice concentrate. With mixer, beat in pudding mix. Chill 10 minutes.

❷ Fold in whipped topping. Spoon into crusts. Chill at least 1 hour.

❸ Cut out 36 tiny waxed paper triangles for eyes and noses; cut out 12 waxed paper mouths. Lightly spray 1 side of each waxed paper cut-out with nonstick coating. Arrange cut-outs on tarts, sprayed sides down, to resemble jack-o'-lanterns.

❹ Shake orange sprinkles over tarts to cover tops. Carefully remove waxed paper shapes. Place a halved gumdrop at top of each tart. Store leftovers covered in refrigerator.

*NOTE: To remove tarts from foil pans, brush crusts with slightly beaten egg white (before filling); bake in 375° oven for 5 minutes. Cool; remove from foil pans. Fill and chill.

Eagle® Brand *tip*

A Touch of "Magic"

Eagle® Brand Sweetened Condensed Milk, made with all-natural milk and sugar, is so rich and creamy that usually recipes don't need eggs, cream or sugar for delicious results. Call on this magic any time of the year for great treats!

Pecan Pie Bars (see recipe, page 40) and Holiday Pumpkin Squares (see recipe opposite page)

Holiday Pumpkin Squares

Next Thanksgiving, offer two favorite flavors—pumpkin and mincemeat—in a new way: dessert squares instead of pies.

Prep Time: 25 minutes   Baking Time: 15 minutes + 15 to 20 minutes
Makes 24 servings

1¼   cups unsifted flour
⅓   cup granulated sugar
⅓   cup firmly packed
     brown sugar
¾   cup butter
1   (15-ounce) can pumpkin
1   (14-ounce) can Eagle® Brand
     Sweetened Condensed Milk
     (NOT evaporated milk)
2   eggs, beaten
1   teaspoon ground cinnamon
½   teaspoon ground allspice
¼   teaspoon salt
1   (27-ounce) jar None Such®
     Ready-to-Use Mincemeat
1   cup chopped walnuts
1   tablespoon unsifted flour

❶ Preheat oven to 375°. In medium-sized bowl, combine 1¼ cups flour and sugars. Cut in butter until crumbly. Set aside 1 cup of the mixture. Pat remaining mixture on bottom of ungreased 13x9-inch baking pan. Bake 15 minutes.

❷ Meanwhile, in large bowl, combine pumpkin, Eagle Brand, eggs, cinnamon, allspice and salt. Carefully spread None Such over partially baked crust. Spoon pumpkin mixture over. Bake 15 minutes. Remove from oven.

❸ Stir nuts and 1 tablespoon flour into reserved crumb mixture. Sprinkle over pumpkin mixture. Bake 15 to 20 minutes longer or until set. Cool slightly. Cut into squares. Serve warm. Store leftovers covered in refrigerator.

Pecan Pie Bars

Make it a festive yet fuss-free Thanksgiving holiday dinner party by serving these easy-to-make bars that are chock-full of pecans (shown on page 39).

Prep Time: 15 minutes   Baking Time: 15 minutes + 25 minutes
Makes 36 bars

- 2 cups unsifted flour
- ¼ cup packed brown sugar
- ½ cup (1 stick) butter
- 1½ cups chopped pecans
- 1 (14-ounce) can Eagle® Brand Original *or* Creamy Chocolate Sweetened Condensed Milk (NOT evaporated milk)
- 3 eggs, beaten
- 2 tablespoons ReaLemon® Lemon Juice from Concentrate

❶ Preheat oven to 350°. In medium-sized bowl, combine flour and brown sugar; cut in butter until crumbly. Press mixture on bottom of ungreased 13x9-inch baking pan. Bake 15 minutes.

❷ Meanwhile, combine pecans, Eagle Brand, eggs and ReaLemon; pour over crust. Bake 25 minutes or until filling is set. Cool. Cut into bars. Store covered at room temperature.

Chocolate Swizzle Nog

Cozy up to the Christmas tree with steaming mugs of this rich, whipped cream-topped treat (shown on page 42).

Prep Time: 5 minutes   Cooking Time: 5 minutes   Makes 4 servings

- 1 (14-ounce) can Eagle® Brand Creamy Chocolate Sweetened Condensed Milk* (NOT evaporated milk)
- 2 cups milk
- ½ teaspoon vanilla extract *or* peppermint extract
- Whipped cream *or* whipped topping

❶ In medium-sized saucepan, combine Eagle Brand and milk. Heat through, stirring constantly. Remove from heat.

❷ Stir in vanilla or peppermint extract. Serve warm in mugs; top with whipped cream or topping.

*NOTE: You can substitute Eagle® Brand Original Sweetened Condensed Milk *plus* 2 tablespoons unsweetened cocoa powder for the Eagle® Brand Creamy Chocolate Sweetened Condensed Milk.

Strawberry Splash Punch

If your New Year's Eve bash is big, make two batches of this pretty-in-pink punch and serve it in a cut-glass punch bowl (shown on pages 20–21).

Prep Time: 10 minutes   Makes 10 servings

1½   cups fresh whole strawberries
½   cup ReaLemon® Lemon Juice from Concentrate, chilled
1   (14-ounce) can Eagle® Brand Sweetened Condensed Milk
     (NOT evaporated milk), chilled
1   (1-liter) bottle strawberry flavored carbonated beverage, chilled
     Ice cubes, optional
     Fresh whole strawberries, optional

❶ In blender container, combine 1½ cups strawberries and ReaLemon; cover and blend until smooth. Add Eagle Brand; cover and blend. Pour into large pitcher. Gradually stir in carbonated beverage. Add ice if desired. Garnish each serving with a whole strawberry if desired.

Eagle® Brand *tip*

Easy Entertaining

If you've always wanted to cap off the holiday season with a festive tree-trimming party or open house, this is the year to do it. Entertaining friends and family doesn't have to mean spending days in the kitchen. Just make three or four kinds of bar cookies from this book. (You can do this weeks ahead and stash them in the freezer.) At party time, mix up a batch of one of the Eagle® Brand beverages from the book *(see the index)* and brew some coffee—refreshments are served.

Peppermint-Filled Yule Log

Reminiscent of a log on a blazing fire, this traditional Christmas cake symbolizes the warmth and hospitality of the holiday season.

Prep Time: 40 minutes   Baking Time: 20 minutes
Freezing Time: 2 hours   Makes 10 servings

    Cake Roll (recipe follows)
3   cups peppermint stick ice cream
1   (14-ounce) can Eagle® Brand Sweetened Condensed Milk
    (NOT evaporated milk)
2   (1-ounce) squares unsweetened chocolate, cut up
3   tablespoons water
½ teaspoon peppermint extract

❶ Prepare Cake Roll.

❷ Stir ice cream just until softened; spread over unrolled cake to ½ inch from edges. Reroll. Diagonally cut 4-inch piece from an end. Place long roll on serving plate; place cut edge of piece against side to resemble branch. Place in freezer while preparing frosting.

❸ For frosting, in heavy saucepan, combine Eagle Brand and chocolate. Cook and stir over medium heat until chocolate melts and mixture thickens, about 6 to 8 minutes. Remove from heat; stir in 3 tablespoons water and peppermint extract. Cook, stirring rapidly, until thickened again, 3 to 4 minutes. Cool 15 minutes or until mixture thickens.

❹ Quickly frost cake; return to freezer for 5 minutes. With fork, score wavy lines in frosting. Freeze at least 2 hours. Remove from freezer 5 minutes before serving.

Cake Roll: Preheat oven to 350°. Well-grease and lightly flour 15x10-inch jelly-roll pan; set aside. With mixer, beat 3 eggs and 1 teaspoon vanilla extract in large bowl 3 to 4 minutes or until fluffy. Gradually beat in 1 cup sugar, about 2 tablespoons at a time. With mixer at low speed, beat in ⅓ cup water. Add 1 cup unsifted flour and ½ teaspoon baking powder; beat at low speed just until combined. Spread batter evenly in the prepared pan. Bake 20 minutes or until cake springs back when lightly touched. Immediately loosen edges from pan; turn cake out onto a towel sprinkled with powdered sugar. Roll up towel and cake, jelly-roll style, starting from a long side. Cool on wire rack. Unroll cake; remove towel.

Decorating Idea: For a festive garnish for your Yule Log, cut holly leaf shapes from green ready-to-use rolled fondant; trace veins into leaves with wooden pick. Arrange leaves and fresh cranberries on log to resemble holly.

Peppermint-Filled Yule Log (see recipe above) and
Chocolate Swizzle Nog (see recipe, page 40)

Treats In RECORD TIME

Short on time but have a serious craving for something sweet? No problem. If you've got 15 minutes, you've got time to make a great dessert, such as Almond Tarts, Chocolate-Caramel Fondue or a refreshing Fruit Smoothie. Each of these tempting treats—and any of the rest of the great recipes in this chapter—can be made in 15 minutes or less for a treat that's sure to satisfy your sweet tooth.

Clockwise from front: Fruit Smoothies, Key Lime Smoothies (see recipes, page 46) and Apple Pie Shake (see recipe, page 47)

Treats In RECORD TiME

Fruit Smoothies

What a way to wake up! This quick-to-fix, strawberry-flavored smoothie will leave you in the pink and ready to have a great day (shown on pages 44–45).

Prep Time: 5 minutes   Makes 5 servings

1 (14-ounce) can Eagle® Brand Sweetened Condensed Milk (NOT evaporated milk)
1 (8-ounce) carton plain yogurt
1 small banana, cut up
1 cup frozen *or* fresh whole strawberries
1 (8-ounce) can crushed pineapple packed with juice, chilled
2 tablespoons ReaLemon® Lemon Juice from Concentrate
1 cup ice cubes
   Halved fresh strawberries, optional

❶ Chill Eagle Brand. In blender container, combine Eagle Brand, yogurt, banana, whole strawberries, pineapple with its juice and ReaLemon; cover and blend until smooth. With blender running, gradually add ice cubes, blending until smooth. Garnish with halved strawberries if desired. Serve immediately.

VARIATIONS

Peach Smoothies: Omit strawberries and pineapple. Add 2 cups frozen *or* fresh sliced peaches. Proceed as above.

Key Lime Smoothies: Omit strawberries, pineapple and ReaLemon. Add ⅓ cup Key lime juice. Proceed as above. Tint with green food coloring if desired. Garnish with lime slices if desired.

Eagle® Brand *tip*

Trim the Fat

Turn Fruit Smoothies (above) into a tasty lowfat treat by substituting Eagle® Brand Fat Free or Low Fat Sweetened Condensed Milk for the original Eagle® Brand and using fat free yogurt. In fact, if you want to trim fat for any of the recipes in this book, just use Eagle® Brand Fat Free or Low Fat Sweetened Condensed Milk instead of original Eagle® Brand.

Mocha Coffee

No need to trek to the local coffeehouse for a warm-up. Stir together this creamy coffee at home—it's a perfect chill-chaser for a fall or winter evening (shown on page 84).

Prep Time: 10 minutes   Makes 2 or 3 servings

2   cups strong brewed coffee
⅔   cup (one-half 14-ounce can)
     Eagle® Brand
     Creamy Chocolate
     Sweetened Condensed Milk
     (NOT evaporated milk)
¼   teaspoon ground cinnamon
     Whipped cream *or* vanilla
        ice cream, optional

❶ In large saucepan, combine coffee, Eagle Brand and cinnamon. Heat through, stirring constantly. Serve in mugs. Top with whipped cream *or* small spoonful of ice cream if desired.

TIP: Use remaining Eagle Brand as dip for fruit or pour into storage container and store tightly covered in refrigerator for up to 1 week.

Apple Pie Shake

A treat for any time of year, this refreshing beverage has the same wonderful flavors of apple pie, but without the crust! It will be your new "comfort food" (shown on pages 44–45).

Prep Time: 5 minutes   Makes 4 or 5 servings

1   (14-ounce) can Eagle® Brand
     Sweetened Condensed Milk
     (NOT evaporated milk)
1   cup applesauce, chilled
½   cup apple juice *or* apple
        cider, chilled
½   teaspoon apple pie spice*
3   cups crushed ice
     Apple wedges and apple
        peel strips, optional

❶ Chill Eagle Brand. In blender container, combine Eagle Brand, applesauce, apple juice and apple pie spice; cover and blend until smooth. With blender running, gradually add ice, blending until smooth. Serve immediately. Garnish with apple wedges and apple peel strips if desired.

*NOTE: Look for apple pie spice in the spice section of your supermarket or substitute a mixture of ¼ teaspoon ground cinnamon, ⅛ teaspoon ground nutmeg and dash ground allspice.

Chocolate-Caramel Fondue

Pound cake cut with tiny heart cutters and bright red berries make festive dippers for this creamy chocolate fondue. Make it anytime!

Prep Time: 15 minutes   Makes 2½ cups

3   (1-ounce) squares unsweetened chocolate, chopped
1   (14-ounce) can Eagle® Brand Sweetened Condensed Milk
      (NOT evaporated milk)
1   (12¼-ounce) jar caramel ice cream topping
      Dippers: Fresh fruit *and/or* cookies, pound cake pieces *or* angel
      food cake pieces

❶ In medium saucepan, melt chocolate with Eagle Brand and caramel topping.

❷ Pour into serving bowl or individual cups. Serve with desired dippers.

Chocolate Cream Crepes

Elegant enough for unexpected company, but easy enough to make for everyday, this double-chocolate dessert starts with purchased crepes (found in the produce section of most large supermarkets).

Prep Time: 10 minutes plus assembling   Chilling Time: 15 minutes
Makes 5 servings

1	(14-ounce) can Eagle® Brand Sweetened Condensed Milk (NOT evaporated milk)
¼	cup cold water
1	(4-serving size) package instant chocolate pudding mix
¼	cup unsweetened cocoa powder
1	cup whipping cream, whipped
1	(4½-ounce) package ready-to-use crepes (10 crepes)
	Sifted powdered sugar
1½	cups sliced *or* cut up fresh fruit, such as strawberries, peaches, nectarines *and/or* kiwi fruit
	White chocolate curls, optional

❶ With mixer, beat Eagle Brand and water in large bowl. Beat in pudding mix and cocoa powder. Fold in whipped cream. Cover and chill 15 minutes.

❷ Pipe or spoon a generous ⅓ cup of filling into center of each crepe. Roll up each crepe. Place on serving plate. Sprinkle with powdered sugar.

❸ Spoon fruit over crepes. Garnish with white chocolate curls if desired.

Super-Simple Sundaes

Chocolate and peanut butter are superbly blended in the creamy sauce for this sundae. It's easy, delicious and sure to become a family favorite!

Prep Time: 15 minutes   Makes 6 servings

2 (1-ounce) squares
    semi-sweet chocolate,
    coarsely chopped
2 tablespoons creamy
    peanut butter
1 (14-ounce) can Eagle® Brand
    Original *or* Creamy Chocolate
    Sweetened Condensed Milk
    (NOT evaporated milk)
2 tablespoons milk
1 teaspoon vanilla extract
1 quart ice cream, any flavor

Toppings: Miniature candy-
    coated semi-sweet
    chocolate candies,
    chopped nuts *and/or*
    whipped topping, optional

❶ For sauce, in medium-sized saucepan, melt chocolate and peanut butter with Eagle Brand and milk over medium-low heat, stirring constantly. Remove from heat; stir in vanilla. Cool slightly.

❷ Scoop ice cream into 6 individual serving bowls. Drizzle with warm sauce. Top with desired toppings.

Trail Blazer Treats

Mix up these crispy, chocolate-peanut-butter-flavored granola bites and tuck them into the refrigerator for a quick after-school snack.

Prep Time: 15 minutes   Chilling Time: 1 to 2 hours   Makes 30 bars

3 (1-ounce) squares
    unsweetened chocolate,
    cut up
¼ cup peanut butter
1 (14-ounce) can Eagle® Brand
    Sweetened Condensed Milk
    (NOT evaporated milk)
1 teaspoon vanilla extract
4½ cups granola cereal
1⅓ cups coconut

❶ In large saucepan, melt chocolate and peanut butter with Eagle Brand. Remove from heat; stir in vanilla. Stir in granola and coconut.

❷ Pat into 13x9-inch baking pan. Chill 1 to 2 hours or until set. Cut into bars. Store leftovers covered in refrigerator.

Almond Tarts

For a dramatic garnish, dust these delicately flavored tarts with chocolate shavings and pile them high with pretty curls of white chocolate and semi-sweet chocolate.

Prep Time: 15 minutes   Chilling Time: 1 hour   Makes 12 tarts

1   (14-ounce) can Eagle® Brand Sweetened Condensed Milk (NOT evaporated milk)
⅔ cup milk
    Few drops almond extract
1   (4-serving size) package instant vanilla pudding mix
4   ounces (one-half 8-ounce container) frozen non-dairy whipped topping, thawed
2   (4-ounce) packages single-serve graham cracker pie crusts*

❶ In large bowl, combine Eagle Brand, milk and almond extract. With mixer, beat in pudding mix. Fold in topping.

❷ Spoon into crusts. Cover and chill at least 1 hour. Refrigerate leftovers.

*NOTE: To remove crusts from foil pans, brush crusts with slightly beaten egg white (before filling); bake in 375° oven 5 minutes. Cool; remove from foil pans. Fill; chill.

Top Bananas with Creamy Sauce

A touch of rum extract is the secret ingredient in this luscious fruit dessert.

Prep Time: 5 minutes   Makes 6 servings

1 (14-ounce) can Eagle® Brand
   Sweetened Condensed Milk
   (NOT evaporated milk)
¼ cup milk
   Several drops rum extract
6 small bananas, peeled and
   sliced
2 tablespoons ReaLemon®
   Lemon Juice from
   Concentrate
3 tablespoons chopped
   toasted pecans

❶ In medium-sized bowl, combine Eagle Brand, milk and rum extract.

❷ In large bowl, toss bananas with ReaLemon. Spoon bananas into 6 dessert dishes. Spoon Eagle Brand mixture over bananas; sprinkle with nuts.

TIP: For banana sundaes, stir bananas into Eagle Brand mixture; spoon over scoops of vanilla *or* chocolate ice cream (or over slices of pound cake *or* angel food cake); sprinkle with nuts.

Kids in the Kitchen

There's no better motivation for getting the kids to spend some time with mom or dad in the kitchen than the promise of a sweet reward. S'more Cookie Pizza, Choose-a-Color Popcorn Treat or a frosty Purple Cow blender drink are just a few of the fun treats kids will love to make with an adult helper. And your reward? A nibble or two of the delicious results, of course—and precious time with your children.

S'more Cookie Pizza (see recipe, page 56)

S'more Cookie Pizza

No need to wait for a campfire to have another s'more. This oven version of the childhood favorite can be made any time (shown on pages 54–55).

Prep Time: 15 minutes   Baking Time: 10 minutes + 4 minutes
Makes 2 pizzas (24 servings)

1 (18-ounce) roll refrigerated sugar-cookie dough
2 cups (12 ounces) semi-sweet chocolate chips
1 (14-ounce) can Eagle® Brand Sweetened Condensed Milk (NOT evaporated milk)
2 cups candy-coated milk chocolate candies
2 cups miniature marshmallows
½ cup peanuts

❶ Preheat oven to 375°. Press cookie dough into 2 ungreased 12-inch pizza pans. Bake 10 minutes or until golden. Remove from oven.

❷ In medium-sized saucepan, melt chips with Eagle Brand. Spread over crusts. Sprinkle with milk chocolate candies, marshmallows and peanuts.

❸ Bake 4 minutes or until marshmallows are lightly toasted. Cool. Cut into wedges.

Surprise-in-a-Pocket Cupcakes

There's a treat inside each of these little cakes—a rich, creamy filling. Ask kids to help you by letting them decorate the tops to suit their fancy.

Prep Time: 40 minutes   Baking Time: 18 minutes   Makes 40

3   eggs
2   (3-ounce) packages cream
      cheese, softened
1   (14-ounce) can Eagle® Brand
      Sweetened Condensed Milk
      (NOT evaporated milk)
1   (18¼- *or* 18½-ounce)
      package chocolate
      cake mix
1⅓   cups water
      Chocolate Frosting
      (recipe follows)
      Suggested Decorations:
      Colored sugar, small
      multicolored decorative
      candies, crushed cookies

❶ Preheat oven to 375°. Line 40 muffin tins with paper bake cups. Separate 1 egg yolk from white. With mixer, beat cream cheese in large bowl until fluffy. Gradually beat in ⅓ cup of the Eagle Brand and egg yolk. Set aside.

❷ In large bowl, combine cake mix, the remaining Eagle Brand, water, 2 eggs and egg white. With mixer, beat on low speed until moistened; beat on high speed for 2 minutes.

❸ Divide batter among prepared muffin tins, filling each ⅔ full. Add a rounded teaspoonful of cream cheese mixture to center of each muffin tin.

❹ Bake 18 minutes or until tops spring back when lightly touched. (Filling will sink during baking.) Cool on wire rack.

❺ Frost cupcakes with Chocolate Frosting; decorate one at a time (do not wait until end to decorate as top of frosting sets quickly). Store at room temperature.

Chocolate Frosting: In heavy medium-sized saucepan, combine 1 (14-ounce) can Eagle® Brand Sweetened Condensed Milk (NOT evaporated milk), 1 cup (6 ounces) semi-sweet chocolate chips and dash salt. Cook and stir over medium heat until chips melt; cook and stir 3 minutes more. Remove from heat; cool 15 minutes. With mixer, beat in 2 cups sifted powdered sugar and 1 teaspoon vanilla extract.

Orange Dream Pops

These frosty orange pops will be the highlight of a hot summer day. All the kids in the neighborhood will want to join in the fun.

Prep Time: 5 minutes   Freezing Time: Overnight   Makes 10 pops

3   cups orange juice *or* refrigerated orange juice blend
1   (14-ounce) can Eagle® Brand Sweetened Condensed Milk (NOT evaporated milk)
¼   cup ReaLemon® Lemon Juice from Concentrate
10   (5-ounce) paper cups (see tip below)
10   wooden sticks

❶ In large bowl, stir together orange juice, Eagle Brand and ReaLemon. Pour into paper cups.

❷ Cover each cup with foil. Make small hole in foil with knife. Insert wooden stick or plastic spoon into each cup through hole. Freeze overnight or until firm. To serve, remove foil; tear off paper.

Eagle® Brand *tip*

WOW! Pops with Pizzazz

Surprise your gang with yummy Orange Dream Pops, frozen in awesome shapes (like those shown on the opposite page). You're sure to win the award for the coolest treats on the block.

• For flat-bottomed pops, use small paper cups.

• To make cone shapes, use paper cups with pointed bottoms (set each cup in a foam cup or juice glass to keep it upright while freezing).

• For special decorative shapes, purchase an assortment of whimsical pop molds.

Choose-a-Color Popcorn Treat

The pot of gold at the end of this rainbow of popcorn is a sweet snack kids can help make in their favorite colors and flavors (shown on page 65).

Prep Time: 10 minutes   Baking Time: 20 minutes   Makes about 16 cups

12   cups unseasoned *or* lightly
      salted popped popcorn
1   (14-ounce) can Eagle® Brand
      Sweetened Condensed Milk
      (NOT evaporated milk)
1   (3-ounce) package cherry-
      flavored gelatin *or* other
      flavored gelatin

❶ Preheat oven to 300°. Line large shallow roasting pan with heavy foil, extending foil over edges of pan. Butter foil. Remove all unpopped kernels from popped popcorn. Pour popcorn into prepared pan. Keep warm in oven.

❷ In medium saucepan, combine Eagle Brand and dry gelatin. Heat and stir over medium heat until mixture is slightly thickened and bubbly, 4 to 5 minutes.

❸ Pour Eagle Brand mixture over popcorn; with long-handled wooden spoon, stir gently to coat. Bake 20 minutes, stirring every 5 minutes. Carefully turn out onto large piece of lightly buttered foil. Cool. Break into pieces or clusters.

Eagle® Brand *tip*

POP! Popcorn Math

Wondering how much popcorn you'll need for Choose-a-Color Popcorn Treat (above)? For air-popped corn, plan on using about ½ cup unpopped kernels (or amount listed on package) for every 4 cups of popped popcorn you need. Or, if you like, purchase already-popped popcorn (without oil) at the supermarket. When preparing or purchasing the popcorn, make sure it is unseasoned or only lightly salted.

And just in case your little helpers need a sample or two of the popped corn before mixing the recipe, pop a little extra corn for sampling.

Dipsy Doodles Butterscotch Dip

The kids will be begging to eat an apple a day—or even a pear or banana—when they can dunk it into this butterscotch fruit dip.

Prep Time: 15 minutes   Makes about 2½ cups dip

1 (4-serving size) cook-before-serving butterscotch pudding mix (NOT instant)

1 (14-ounce) can Eagle® Brand Sweetened Condensed Milk (NOT evaporated milk)

1½ cups milk

Apples *or* pears, cored and sliced, *or* banana chunks

❶ In medium-sized saucepan, combine pudding mix, Eagle Brand and milk. Cook and stir until thickened and bubbly; cook 2 minutes more. Cool slightly. Pour into serving bowl or individual cups. Serve warm with fruit.

TIP: Store leftovers covered in the refrigerator. Reheat and serve as a sauce over vanilla ice cream. Sprinkle sauce with miniature semi-sweet chocolate chips or toasted nuts if desired.

Peanut Butter Paradise Ice Cream

Peanut butter sandwiches are good, and peanut butter cookies are great, but peanut butter ice cream with peanut butter candy? It's dandy!

Prep Time: 15 minutes   Freezing Time: 6 hours   Makes 16 servings

- 1 (14-ounce) can Eagle® Brand Creamy Chocolate Sweetened Condensed Milk (NOT evaporated milk)
- 1 (10-ounce) package miniature candy-coated peanut butter flavored candies
- ½ cup peanut butter
- 3 cups (1½ pints) whipping cream

❶ In large bowl, combine Eagle Brand, candy pieces and peanut butter; set aside.

❷ Pour whipping cream into chilled large bowl. With mixer, beat whipping cream to soft peaks. Gradually fold into Eagle Brand mixture. Transfer to large freezer container. Cover tightly and freeze 6 hours or until firm.

❸ Remove from freezer 15 minutes before serving.

Banana-Fanana Splits

Invite friends over, set out the ingredients and let them make banana splits!

Prep Time: 20 minutes   Makes 5 to 6 large servings or 10 to 12 small servings

- 1 (1-ounce) square unsweetened chocolate, cut up
- 1 (14-ounce) can Eagle® Brand Sweetened Condensed Milk (NOT evaporated milk)
- 1 tablespoon milk
- ¼ teaspoon vanilla extract
- ¾ cup coarsely chopped strawberries
- 1 tablespoon ReaLemon® Lemon Juice from Concentrate
- 5 *or* 6 large bananas, peeled and halved lengthwise
- 1 pint chocolate ice cream
- 1 pint vanilla ice cream
- 1 pint strawberry ice cream

Toppings: **Pressurized whipped topping, chopped nuts** *and/or* **maraschino cherries**

❶ For chocolate sauce, in medium-sized saucepan, melt chocolate with ⅔ cup (one-half 14-ounce can) of the Eagle Brand and milk. Remove from heat; stir in vanilla. Cool.

❷ For strawberry sauce, combine remaining one-half can Eagle Brand, strawberries and ReaLemon.

❸ In banana split dishes or individual serving dishes, arrange bananas and scoops of ice cream. Drizzle with chocolate sauce and strawberry sauce. Top with toppings as desired. Serve immediately.

Banana-Fanana Splits (see recipe above)

Rocky Roadsters

Marshmallows and nuts are the tasty "rocks" in these chocolate bar cookies.

Prep Time: 10 minutes   Baking Time: 20 to 25 minutes   Makes 30 to 36 bars

¼ cup butter *or* margarine
15 to 18 chocolate graham cracker squares (2½-inch squares)
1 (11½-ounce) package milk chocolate chips
1 cup miniature marshmallows
½ cup chopped walnuts
1 (14-ounce) can Eagle® Brand Sweetened Condensed Milk (NOT evaporated milk)

❶ Preheat oven to 350°. Line 13x9-inch baking pan with foil, extending foil over edges of pan. In foil-lined pan, melt butter in oven.

❷ Arrange graham cracker squares in pan, breaking them if necessary to cover bottom of pan. Top with chocolate chips, marshmallows and walnuts in order listed. Pour Eagle Brand evenly over all.

❸ Bake 20 to 25 minutes or until marshmallows are golden and Eagle Brand bubbles over entire surface. Cool. Lift foil to remove from pan. Cut into bars.

Purple Cows

Take your kids or grandkids on a nostalgia trip when you whip up this version of the creamy, sweet and purple soda shop treat.

Prep Time: 10 minutes   Makes 2 to 4 servings

1 (14-ounce) can Eagle® Brand Sweetened Condensed Milk (NOT evaporated milk)
6 ounces (one-half 12-ounce can) frozen grape juice concentrate
1 cup vanilla frozen yogurt
2 cups ice cubes
  Pressurized whipped topping *and/or* decorative sprinkles

❶ In blender container, combine Eagle Brand and juice concentrate. Add frozen yogurt; cover and blend until smooth.

❷ With blender running, add ice cubes, one at a time, blending until smooth. Pour into tall glasses. Top with whipped topping and/or decorative sprinkles.

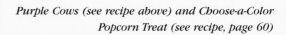

Purple Cows (see recipe above) and Choose-a-Color Popcorn Treat (see recipe, page 60)

Sweet & Simple Treats

Whether you want to celebrate a sunny day or cheer up a gloomy day, here's a host of treats that will make your day joyful. Maybe it's Chocolate Chip and Nut Tart for a delicious ending to a quiet dinner or Fudge Swirl Supreme Ice Cream for a scrumptious treat on a summer afternoon. These and all of the other easy recipes in this chapter add a bit of sweetness to life's little moments.

Chocolate Chip and Nut Tart (see recipe, page 68) and Fudge Swirl Supreme Ice Cream (see recipe, page 71)

Chocolate Chip and Nut Tart

This impressive, yet easy-to-make tart is the perfect choice for a dessert party. Chock-full of nuts and chocolate, it will satisfy even the sweetest tooth (shown on pages 66–67).

Prep Time: 25 minutes   Baking Time: 35 minutes   Makes 12 servings

1   folded refrigerated unbaked pie crust (one-half 15-ounce package)
3   eggs, beaten
1   (14-ounce) can Eagle® Brand Sweetened Condensed Milk
      (NOT evaporated milk)
2   tablespoons butter *or* margarine, melted
1   cup coarsely chopped salted mixed nuts
¾   cup miniature semi-sweet chocolate chips
2   teaspoons shortening

❶ Let refrigerated pie crust stand at room temperature according to package directions. Preheat oven to 350°. On a floured surface, roll pie crust from center to edge, forming a circle about 12 inches in diameter. Ease pastry into 11-inch tart pan with removable bottom. Trim pastry even with the rim of the pan.

❷ For filling, combine eggs, Eagle Brand and melted butter. Stir in nuts and ½ cup of the chips. Place the pastry-lined tart pan on a baking sheet on the oven rack. Carefully pour filling into pan. Bake 35 minutes or until a knife inserted near the center comes out clean. Cool.

❸ To serve, in small saucepan, melt remaining chips and shortening over low heat. Drizzle over tart. Store leftovers covered in refrigerator.

Eagle® Brand *tip*

Pie Pastry Choices

When there's little time to make pie crust from scratch, the supermarket offers several work-saving options.

• In the baking aisle, you'll find graham cracker and chocolate flavored crumb crusts as well as pastry mixes in 1-crust and 2-crust sizes.

• In the dairy case, look for packages of refrigerated pastry that contain two 12-inch crusts that are already rolled out and ready to ease into a pie plate.

• In the freezer case, look for deep-dish frozen unbaked crusts. (Be sure to select a package that's marked "deep dish" so it will hold the same amount of filling as a homemade crust.)

Ambrosia Freeze

Ambrosia—the darling fruit dessert of the 1960s—is back, but with a '90s twist: It's frosty and frozen and easier to make than ever!

Prep Time: 10 minutes   Freezing Time: 6 hours   Makes 8 to 10 servings

1   (8-ounce) tub cream cheese with strawberries
2   medium-sized ripe bananas
1   (14-ounce) can Eagle® Brand Sweetened Condensed Milk
      (NOT evaporated milk)
1   (8-ounce) carton low-fat strawberry yogurt
2   tablespoons ReaLemon® Lemon Juice from Concentrate
1   (11-ounce) can mandarin orange sections, drained
1   (8-ounce) can crushed pineapple, drained
½   cup toasted flaked coconut
     Several drops red food coloring, optional

❶ With mixer, beat cream cheese and bananas in large bowl until nearly smooth. Beat in Eagle Brand, yogurt and ReaLemon. Stir in orange sections, pineapple and coconut. Stir in food coloring if desired. Spoon into 11x7-inch baking dish. Cover and freeze 6 hours or until firm.

❷ Remove from freezer 15 minutes before serving. Cut into pieces; serve in dessert dishes.

Piña Colada Cream Dessert

Pineapple, lime and coconut are featured in this tropical-flavored dessert.

Prep Time: 10 minutes   Freezing Time: 2 hours + 6 hours
Makes 6 to 8 servings

1 (14-ounce) can Eagle® Brand Sweetened Condensed Milk (NOT evaporated milk)
1 cup milk
½ cup frozen pineapple juice concentrate, thawed
2 tablespoons ReaLime® Lime Juice from Concentrate
¾ cup toasted flaked coconut
   Edible flowers, optional

❶ Combine Eagle Brand, milk, pineapple juice concentrate and ReaLime. Transfer to 9x9-inch baking pan. Cover; freeze 2 hours or until almost firm.

❷ Break frozen mixture into small chunks; transfer to chilled large bowl. With mixer, beat until smooth but not melted. Stir in coconut. Return to pan. Cover; freeze 6 hours or until firm. To serve, scoop into dessert dishes. Garnish with flowers if desired.

Fudge Swirl Supreme Ice Cream

Only four ingredients are needed for this chocolate-and-vanilla masterpiece (shown on pages 66–67).

Prep Time: 35 minutes   Freezing Time: 1½ hours + 3 hours
Makes 6 to 8 servings

2 cups (1 pint) whipping cream
1 (14-ounce) can Eagle® Brand Sweetened Condensed Milk (NOT evaporated milk)
½ teaspoon vanilla extract
1 cup (6-ounces) semi-sweet chocolate chips
   Fresh raspberries, optional

❶ In large bowl, combine cream, ½ cup of the Eagle Brand and vanilla. Cover; chill 30 minutes. With mixer, beat until soft peaks form. Spoon into 8-inch square baking pan. Cover; freeze 1½ hours or until partially frozen.

❷ In saucepan, melt chips with remaining Eagle Brand. Cool 15 minutes; swirl into partially frozen mixture. Cover; freeze 3 hours or until firm. Remove from freezer 10 minutes before serving. Serve with raspberries if desired.

Piña Colada Cream Dessert
(see recipe above)

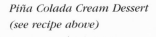

Café au Lait Ice Cream

Attention coffee-lovers: Serve this creamy, nut-studded coffee ice cream with a fresh pot of hot java. (You can never have too much, can you?)

Prep Time: 20 minutes   Freezing Time: 4 hours
Makes 8 to 10 servings

½ cup hot water
4 teaspoons instant
       coffee crystals
2 cups (1 pint) whipping cream
1 (14-ounce) can Eagle® Brand
       Sweetened Condensed Milk
       (NOT evaporated milk)
¼ teaspoon almond extract
½ cup toasted chopped
       pecans *or* almonds,
       optional

❶ In large bowl, stir water and coffee crystals until dissolved; cool. Add whipping cream, Eagle Brand and almond extract.

❷ With mixer, beat 7 minutes or until light and fluffy (mixture will mound but not hold peaks). Fold in nuts if desired. Spoon into 8-inch square baking pan or 9x5-inch loaf pan. Cover; freeze 4 hours or until firm. To serve, scoop into dessert dishes.

Eagle® Brand *tip*

Sundae "Magic"

Improvise your own sensational sundaes by starting with Café au Lait Ice Cream (above) or any of the other irresistible ice creams in this book and topping it with a drizzle of one of the following:

- Super-Simple Sundaes sauce (see recipe, page 50)

- Chocolate-Caramel Fondue (see recipe, page 48)

- Dipsy Doodles Butterscotch Dip (see recipe, page 61)

Finish off your creation with a swirl of whipped cream or whipped topping, some chopped nuts and a bright red maraschino cherry.

White Chocolate Bread Pudding

Great for holiday time—or any time you have leftover French bread—this indulgent bread pudding bejeweled with dried fruit is a true treat.

Prep Time: 20 minutes   Baking Time: 40 to 50 minutes
Makes 10 servings

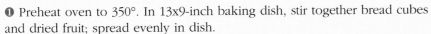

    8   cups dry French bread cubes*
    ½   cup dried tart cherries, dried cranberries, dried blueberries, raisins
          or dried currants
    4   (1-ounce) squares white chocolate *or* 4 ounces white baking bar
  2½   cups water
    1   (14-ounce) can Eagle® Brand Sweetened Condensed Milk
          (NOT evaporated milk)
    3   eggs, beaten
    2   tablespoons butter *or* margarine, melted
    2   tablespoons ReaLemon® Lemon Juice from Concentrate

❶ Preheat oven to 350°. In 13x9-inch baking dish, stir together bread cubes and dried fruit; spread evenly in dish.

❷ In heavy small saucepan, melt white chocolate over very low heat, stirring constantly. In large bowl, combine water, Eagle Brand, eggs, melted butter, ReaLemon and melted white chocolate; pour evenly over bread cubes. With spoon, press bread down to moisten completely.

❸ Bake 40 to 50 minutes or until knife inserted in center comes out clean. Serve warm or let cool. Store leftovers covered in refrigerator.

*NOTE: To make dry bread cubes, preheat oven to 300°. Cut bread into ½-inch-thick slices; cut slices into ½-inch square pieces. Spread in single layer in 15x10-inch baking pan. Bake 10 to 15 minutes or until dry, stirring twice. Cool. Bread will continue to dry and crisp as it cools. (Or, loosely cover bread cubes. Let stand at room temperature 8 to 12 hours; turn once.)

traditions
with a twist

Creamy Cinnamon Rolls

These cinnamon rolls are so simple they don't require a lazy, linger-longer Saturday morning to make. Serve them with your favorite coffee or tea.

Prep Time: 20 minutes
Baking Time: 30 to 35 minutes
Makes 12 rolls

Chilling Time: Overnight
Cooling Time: 5 minutes

2	(1-pound) loaves frozen bread dough, thawed
⅔	cup (one-half 14-ounce can) Eagle® Brand Sweetened Condensed Milk (NOT evaporated milk)
1	cup chopped pecans
2	teaspoons ground cinnamon
1	cup sifted powdered sugar
½	teaspoon vanilla extract
	Chopped pecans, optional

❶ On a lightly floured surface roll each of the bread dough loaves to a 12x9-inch rectangle. Spread ⅓ cup of the Eagle Brand over dough rectangles. Sprinkle with 1 cup pecans and cinnamon. Roll up jelly-roll style starting from a short side. Cut each into 6 slices.

❷ Generously grease 13x9-inch baking pan. Place rolls, cut sides down, in pan. Cover loosely with greased waxed paper and then with plastic wrap. Chill overnight. Cover and chill remaining ⅓ cup Eagle Brand.

❸ To bake, let pan of rolls stand at room temperature for 30 minutes. Preheat oven to 350°. Bake 30 to 35 minutes or until golden brown. Cool in pan 5 minutes; loosen edges and remove rolls from pan.

❹ Meanwhile for frosting, in small bowl, combine powdered sugar, remaining ⅓ cup Eagle Brand and vanilla. Drizzle frosting on warm rolls. Sprinkle with additional chopped pecans if desired.

TIP: Use remaining Eagle Brand as dip for fruit or pour into storage container and store tightly covered in refrigerator for up to 1 week.

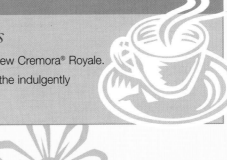

Eagle® Brand *tip*

Attention Coffee Lovers

Perk up your morning coffee with New Cremora® Royale. This premium non-dairy creamer adds the indulgently rich taste of cream to your coffee.

Layered Cheesecake Bars

These distinctive layered bar cookies feature a buttery walnut crust.

Prep Time: 30 minutes   Baking Time: 30 to 35 minutes
Cooling Time: 30 minutes   Makes 24 bars

1	(9-ounce) package None Such® Condensed Mincemeat
1½	cups water
2	cups unsifted flour
½	cup finely chopped walnuts
½	cup (1 stick) butter
1	(14-ounce) can Eagle® Brand Sweetened Condensed Milk (NOT evaporated milk)
4	(3-ounce) packages cream cheese, softened
2	eggs
24	walnut halves *or* chopped walnuts

❶ Preheat oven to 350°. Crumble None Such into medium-sized saucepan. Add water. Bring to boiling; boil gently for 1 minute. Remove from heat. In medium-sized bowl, stir together flour and ½ cup walnuts; set aside.

❷ With mixer, beat butter in large bowl 30 seconds; gradually beat in ⅓ cup of the Eagle Brand. Beat in flour-walnut mixture until crumbly. Press on bottom of 13x9-inch baking pan. Spread with cooled mincemeat.

❸ In another bowl, beat cream cheese with mixer until fluffy. Gradually beat in remaining Eagle Brand and eggs; carefully pour over mincemeat. Top with walnut halves or additional chopped walnuts. Bake 30 to 35 minutes or until top is set. Cool 30 minutes. Cover and chill. Remove from refrigerator 15 minutes before serving. Cut into bars. Store leftovers covered in refrigerator.

Choco-Toffee Sweet-Tooth Treats

Half bar-cookie, half confection, these sweets are 100 percent perfection!

Prep Time: 20 minutes   Baking Time: 20 to 25 minutes

Makes 48 to 60 bars

- ¾ cup (1½ sticks) butter
- 2 cups packed brown sugar
- 1 teaspoon baking soda
- 2 eggs
- 2 teaspoons vanilla extract
- 2½ cups unsifted flour
- 3 cups rolled oats
- 1 (14-ounce) can Eagle® Brand Creamy Chocolate Sweetened Condensed Milk (NOT evaporated milk)
- ½ cup almond brickle pieces, chopped chocolate-covered toffee bars *or* chopped nuts

❶ Preheat oven to 350°. With mixer, beat butter in large bowl 30 seconds. Beat in brown sugar and baking soda, scraping side of bowl occasionally. Beat in eggs and 1 teaspoon of the vanilla. Beat in as much of the flour as you can with the mixer.

❷ Stir in remaining flour and oats. Press ⅔ of the rolled oat mixture on bottom of 15x10-inch baking pan.

❸ For filling, stir together Eagle Brand and remaining vanilla. Spread filling evenly over oat mixture. Stir almond brickle pieces into remaining oat mixture; with spoon, dot over filling.

❹ Bake 20 to 25 minutes or until the top is lightly browned. Cool. Cut into bars. Store covered at room temperature.

TIP: For triangle-shaped bar cookies, cut baked cookies into squares; cut each square diagonally to form triangles.

Chocolate Peanut Butter Bars

These yummy bars get a double dose of peanuts—first from the peanut butter chips in the filling and then from the crunchy peanuts on top.

Prep Time: 15 minutes **Baking Time: 35 minutes** **Makes 32 bars**

1 cup (2 sticks) butter
½ cup packed brown sugar
¼ teaspoon salt
2 cups unsifted flour
1 cup peanut butter flavored chips
1 (14-ounce) can Eagle® Brand Creamy Chocolate Sweetened Condensed Milk (NOT evaporated milk)
1 cup chopped peanuts
1 teaspoon vanilla extract

❶ Preheat oven to 350°. With mixer, beat butter in large bowl 30 seconds. Beat in brown sugar and salt. Beat in flour. Press mixture on bottom of 13x9-inch baking pan.

❷ In medium-sized saucepan, melt chips with Eagle Brand. Stir in ½ cup of the peanuts and vanilla. Spread hot mixture over crust. Sprinkle with remaining peanuts; press down with fork.

❸ Bake 35 minutes or until set in center. Cool. Cut into bars. Store covered at room temperature.

great after school snack

Heaven Scent Baked Apples

These nutmeg-spiced baked apples are the perfect ending to any meal.

Prep Time: 10 minutes   Baking Time: 40 to 45 minutes   Makes 6 servings

6   medium baking apples
    (about 2 pounds), such as
    Rome Beauty *or* York
    Imperial
⅓   cup mixed dried fruit bits
    or raisins
1   (14-ounce) can Eagle® Brand
    Sweetened Condensed Milk
    (NOT evaporated milk)
1   tablespoon water
¼   teaspoon ground nutmeg

❶ Preheat oven to 350°. Core apples; peel a strip from the top of each. If necessary cut thin slice from bottom of each apple so apple will stand upright. Place apples upright in greased 11x7-inch baking dish. Fill centers with fruit bits or raisins.

❷ In medium-sized bowl, combine Eagle Brand, water and nutmeg; pour over and around apples. Set dish in a 13x9-inch pan. Set on oven rack. Carefully pour boiling water into pan to 1-inch depth. Bake 40 to 45 minutes or until apples are tender, occasionally spooning Eagle Brand mixture in bottom of dish over apples. Serve warm.

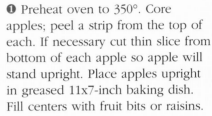

Gifts from the Heart

Want to say "thank you" from the bottom of your heart? Chocolate-Orange Fudge or Cappuccino Caramels Royale will do the trick. How about "Happy Housewarming?" Welcome Home Chocolate Bars are a sure bet. On these pages, you'll find recipes for these easy treats and other homemade candies and cookies, along with creative ideas on how to package them.

Clockwise from front: Chocolate-Orange Fudge (see recipe, page 82), Peanut Butter Fudge (see recipe, page 82) and Cappuccino Caramels Royale (see recipe, page 83)

Gifts from the Heart

Chocolate-Orange Fudge

Chocolate and orange are classic flavor companions, and never more elegantly than in this rich, aromatic fudge (shown on pages 80–81).

Prep Time: 15 minutes   Chilling Time: 2 hours
Makes 36 to 49 pieces (about 1½ pounds)

2½ cups (15 ounces) semi-sweet chocolate chips
1 (14-ounce) can Eagle® Brand Sweetened Condensed Milk (NOT evaporated milk)
½ cup chopped macadamia nuts, almonds *or* pecans, optional
2 teaspoons finely shredded orange peel

❶ Line 8-inch square pan with foil, extending foil over edges of pan. Butter foil; set aside.

❷ In medium-sized saucepan, melt chips with Eagle Brand. Remove from heat; stir in nuts if desired and orange peel. Pour into prepared pan. Cool slightly. Cover and chill 2 hours or until firm.

❸ When firm, use foil to lift out of pan. Cut into diamonds or squares. Store tightly covered in refrigerator.

Peanut Butter Fudge

White chocolate blended with peanut butter creates a deliciously creamy treat (shown on pages 80–81).

Prep Time: 20 minutes   Chilling Time: 2 hours
Makes 64 pieces (about 2¼ pounds)

1 (14-ounce) can Eagle® Brand Sweetened Condensed Milk (NOT evaporated milk)
½ cup creamy peanut butter
2 (6-ounce) packages white chocolate squares *or* white baking bars, chopped
¾ cup chopped peanuts
1 teaspoon vanilla extract

❶ Line 8-inch square pan with foil, extending foil over edges. Butter foil; set aside. In large saucepan, heat Eagle Brand and peanut butter over medium heat until just bubbly, stirring constantly. Remove from heat. Stir in white chocolate until smooth. Immediately stir in peanuts and vanilla.

❷ Pour into prepared pan; spread evenly. Cool. Cover and chill 2 hours or until firm. Use foil to lift candy out of pan. Sprinkle with additional chopped peanuts if desired. Cut into squares. Store leftovers covered in refrigerator.

Cappuccino Caramels Royale

Each buttery, chewy bite of these caramels is accented with the warm flavor of coffee (shown on pages 80–81).

Prep Time: 15 minutes   Cooking Time: 15 to 20 minutes
Makes 64 pieces (about 3 pounds)

1	cup (2 sticks) butter
2¼	cups packed brown sugar
1	(14-ounce) can Eagle® Brand Creamy Chocolate Sweetened Condensed Milk (NOT evaporated milk)
1	cup light corn syrup
1	tablespoon instant coffee crystals
1	cup chopped pecans *or* walnuts, optional

❶ Line 8-inch square baking pan with foil, extending foil over edges of pan. Butter foil; set aside.

❷ In heavy 3-quart saucepan, melt 1 cup butter. Stir in brown sugar, Eagle Brand, corn syrup and coffee crystals. Clip candy thermometer to side of pan. Cook over medium heat, stirring constantly, until thermometer registers 248° (firm-ball stage*). Mixture should boil at moderate, steady rate over entire surface. Reaching firm-ball stage should take 15 to 20 minutes.

❸ Remove from heat. Remove thermometer. Immediately stir in nuts if desired. Quickly pour into prepared pan, spreading evenly with spoon. Cool.

❹ When candy is firm, use foil to lift candy out of pan. Use buttered knife to cut into squares. Wrap each square in plastic wrap or place in candy cups if desired.

*NOTE: To test for firm-ball stage, spoon a few drops of the hot caramel mixture into a cup of very cold (but not icy) water. Using your fingers, form the drops into a ball. Remove ball from water. If it is firm enough to hold its shape but quickly flattens at room temperature, it has reached firm-ball stage. If the mixture hasn't reached the correct stage, continue cooking and retesting, using fresh water and a clean spoon each time.

for being a
good friend

Decadent Chocolate Truffles

These indulgent chocolate truffles can be dressed up however suits your fancy: with nuts, coconut, decorative sprinkles, cocoa powder, powdered sugar, frosting or colored sugar. They're great to serve individually or wrapped up as a gift.

Prep Time: 10 minutes plus shaping and decorating
Chilling Time: 2 to 3 hours   Makes about 6 dozen

- **3   cups (18 ounces) semi-sweet chocolate chips**
- **1   (14-ounce) can Eagle® Brand Original *or* Creamy Chocolate Sweetened Condensed Milk (NOT evaporated milk)**
- **1   tablespoon vanilla extract**
  Coatings: Finely chopped toasted nuts, flaked coconut, chocolate sprinkles, colored sprinkles, unsweetened cocoa powder, sifted powdered sugar *or* colored sugars, optional
  Purchased frosting *or* tiny candies, optional

❶ In large saucepan, melt chips with Eagle Brand. Remove from heat; stir in vanilla. Pour into medium-sized bowl. Cover and chill 2 to 3 hours or until firm.

❷ Shape into 1-inch balls; roll in desired coating and/or decorate with frosting and candies. Store tightly covered in refrigerator.

VARIATION

Cherry-Almond Truffles: Substitute milk chocolate chips for semi-sweet chocolate chips. Add 1⅓ cups toasted coconut and ⅔ cup finely chopped dried tart cherries with the vanilla. Proceed as above. Roll in 1¼ cups finely chopped toasted almonds.

Eagle® Brand *tip*

Toasting Nuts and Coconut

Toasted nuts and coconut give foods a pleasant crunchiness and enhance the food's nutty flavor. To toast, spread the chopped nuts or coconut in a single layer in a shallow baking pan. Preheat oven to 350°. Bake 5 to 10 minutes or until light golden, stirring frequently to prevent burning.

Decadent Chocolate Truffles (see recipe above)
and Mocha Coffee (see recipe, page 47)

Chocolate-Nut Bars

Take your choice of cashews or peanuts for these rich chocolate-topped bars.

Prep Time: 20 minutes   Baking Time: 12 minutes + 10 to 12 minutes
Makes 36 bars

½   cup (1 stick) butter
½   cup sugar
1   cup cashews *or* peanuts
1¼ cups unsifted flour
1   (14-ounce) can Eagle® Brand Sweetened Condensed Milk (NOT evaporated milk)
2   tablespoons butter
2   teaspoons vanilla extract
1   cup (6 ounces) milk chocolate chips

❶ Preheat oven to 350°. With mixer, beat ½ cup butter and sugar in medium-sized bowl. Finely chop ¼ cup of the cashews. Stir chopped cashews and flour into beaten mixture. Press on bottom of 13x9-inch baking pan. Bake

12 minutes. Coarsely chop remaining cashews; set aside.

❷ In heavy saucepan, heat Eagle Brand and 2 tablespoons butter over medium heat until bubbly, stirring constantly. Cook and stir 5 minutes more. (Mixture will thicken and become smooth.) Remove from heat. Stir in vanilla. Carefully spoon over baked layer; bake 10 to 12 minutes or until golden.

❸ Immediately sprinkle with chips. Let stand 2 minutes; spread chocolate evenly over top. Sprinkle with coarsely chopped cashews. Cool; chill to set up chocolate. Cut into bars. Store leftovers covered in refrigerator.

Coconut-Pecan Bar Cookies

Treat your co-workers to these chocolate-covered, chocolate-crusted bars.

Prep Time: 15 minutes   Baking Time: 12 minutes + 18 to 20 minutes
Makes 36 to 48 bars

1¼ cups unsifted flour
¾   cup sugar
¼   cup unsweetened cocoa powder
1   teaspoon baking powder
⅔   cup butter
2   eggs, slightly beaten
1   (14-ounce) can Eagle® Brand Sweetened Condensed Milk (NOT evaporated milk)

1⅓ cups (one-half 7-ounce package) flaked coconut
1   cup chopped pecans
½   cup (3 ounces) semi-sweet chocolate chips, optional
1   teaspoon solid shortening, optional

❶ Preheat oven to 350°. For crust, in large bowl, combine flour, sugar, cocoa powder and baking powder. Cut in butter until crumbly.

Chocolate-Nut Bars and Coconut-Pecan Bar Cookies (see recipes opposite page)

❷ Press mixture on bottom of ungreased 13x9-inch baking pan. Bake for 12 minutes. Remove from oven; let cool slightly.

❸ For filling, in medium-sized bowl, combine eggs, Eagle Brand, coconut and pecans.

Pour over partially-baked crust. Bake 18 to 20 minutes or until set in center. Cool. Cut into bars.

❹ In small saucepan, melt chips with shortening if desired. Drizzle over bars. Store loosely covered at room temperature.

Special Senti-Mint Bars

Leave one of these elegant treats—along with a handwritten note bidding "Sweet Dreams"—by the bedside of an overnight guest.

Prep Time: 20 minutes   Baking Time: 15 minutes + 15 minutes
Makes 40 bars

- 1 (14-ounce) can Eagle® Brand Sweetened Condensed Milk (NOT evaporated milk)
- 2 cups (12 ounces) semi-sweet chocolate chips
- ½ cup (1 stick) butter
- 3 eggs, beaten
- 1¼ cups unsifted flour
- 2 teaspoons baking powder
- ¼ teaspoon baking soda
- 1 cup chopped walnuts, optional
- 2 tablespoons milk
- ¾ teaspoon mint extract
   Mint-chocolate wafers, shaved, optional

❶ Preheat oven to 350°. Set aside ½ cup of the Eagle Brand and 1 cup of the chocolate chips.

❷ For batter, in small saucepan, melt remaining chips with remaining Eagle Brand. Remove from heat and set aside to cool slightly.

❸ With mixer, beat butter in large bowl 30 seconds. Beat in chocolate mixture and eggs. Beat in flour, baking powder and soda. Stir in walnuts if desired. Spread in greased 13x9-inch baking pan. Bake 15 minutes.

❹ Meanwhile, in small saucepan, melt reserved chips with reserved Eagle Brand and milk. Remove from heat; stir in mint extract. Carefully spread over partially-baked mixture. Bake 15 minutes. Cool. Garnish with shaved mint-chocolate wafers if desired. Cut into bars. Store covered at room temperature.

how to say "I love you"

Welcome Home Chocolate Bars

Bake a batch of these easy-to-make chocolate and peanut butter chip bars as a gift for a friend just home from the hospital or a college student coming home for the holidays (shown on cover).

Prep Time: 10 minutes   Baking Time: 25 to 30 minutes   Makes 24 bars

½   cup (1 stick) butter *or* margarine

1½   cups graham cracker crumbs

1   (14-ounce) can Eagle® Brand Sweetened Condensed Milk (NOT evaporated milk)

1   cup (6 ounces) semi-sweet chocolate chips*

1   cup (6 ounces) peanut butter flavored chips*

❶ Preheat oven to 350°. In 13x9-inch baking pan, melt butter in oven.

❷ Sprinkle crumbs evenly over butter; pour Eagle Brand evenly over crumbs. Top with remaining ingredients; press down firmly with spoon.

❸ Bake 25 to 30 minutes or until lightly browned. Cool. Cut into bars. Store covered at room temperature.

***NOTE:** You may substitute butterscotch flavored chips *or* white chocolate chips for the semi-sweet chocolate chips and/or peanut butter chips.

Eagle® Brand *tip*

Wonderful Wrap-Ups

Enchant everyone on your gift list with tantalizing homemade cookies and/or candies packaged in a unique way.

• Festive plates or trays—from paper to the fanciest china—make ideal serving platters. Stack the treats high, overwrap with plastic wrap and tie on eye-catching bows.

• Tuck candies or small cookies into paper liners and arrange them in shallow decorative boxes—star- or heart-shaped ones are especially pretty.

• Baskets or crockery bowls also make captivating containers. Line the baskets or bowls with colorful napkins and pile them with treats.

• Large, wide-mouth canning jars work well, too. Fill them to the brim and slip rounds of colorful cloth between the lids and the metal screw bands.

Raspberry Swirl Cheesecakes

This decadent recipe makes two cheesecakes—one to give as a gift and another to serve your family.

Prep Time: 15 minutes   Baking Time: 25 minutes
Chilling Time: 4 hours   Makes 16 servings

1½ cups fresh *or* thawed lightly sweetened loose-pack frozen red raspberries
1 (14-ounce) can Eagle® Brand Sweetened Condensed Milk (NOT evaporated milk)
2 (8-ounce) packages cream cheese, softened
3 eggs
2 (6-ounce) purchased chocolate flavored crumb pie crusts
  Chocolate and white chocolate leaves (see tip below), optional
  Fresh raspberries, optional

❶ Preheat oven to 350°. In blender container, blend 1½ cups raspberries until smooth; press through sieve to remove seeds. Stir ⅓ cup of the Eagle Brand into sieved raspberries; set aside.

❷ With mixer, beat cream cheese, eggs and remaining Eagle Brand in large bowl. Spoon into crusts. Drizzle with raspberry mixture. With table knife, gently swirl raspberry mixture through cream cheese mixture. Bake 25 minutes or until center is nearly set when shaken. Cool. Cover; chill at least 4 hours. Garnish with chocolate leaves and fresh raspberries if desired. Store leftovers covered in refrigerator.

Eagle® Brand *tip*

Charming Chocolate Leaves

Chocolate leaves are an elegant dessert garnish.

• Start by melting 1 (1-ounce) square semi-sweet chocolate. To melt the chocolate in a microwave oven, place it in a microwave-safe bowl. Heat on 100% power (high) for 1 to 2 minutes or until soft enough to stir smooth, stirring every minute.

• With a small, clean paintbrush, paint several coats of melted chocolate on the undersides of nontoxic leaves, such as mint, lemon or strawberry. Wipe off any chocolate from top sides of leaves. Place leaves, chocolate sides up, on waxed-paper-lined baking sheet or on curved surface, such as rolling pin.

• Refrigerate leaves until chocolate is firm.

• To use, carefully peel leaves away from chocolate.

EAGLE BRAND

Basics

For more than 140 years, cooks have depended on all-natural Eagle® Brand to help them create sweet treats. There are four kinds of Eagle® Brand. Each version provides the rich, creamy base that's the secret for making great desserts and beverages.

Cooking with Eagle® Brand

Eagle® Brand is a special blend of milk and sugar that is condensed by a unique vacuum process. Eagle® Brand is completely different from evaporated milk. Evaporated milk cannot be substituted for Eagle® Brand in recipes.

Most recipes that use Eagle® Brand require no additional sugar because it contains sugar which has been thoroughly dissolved during manufacturing.

Eagle® Brand also has a magical thickening quality. When it's combined with acidic fruit juice, such as lemon juice, it thickens—without heating—to form velvety pie fillings, puddings and other desserts.

Measuring Eagle® Brand

• To measure Eagle® Brand, remove the entire lid and scrape the Eagle® Brand into a glass measuring cup using a rubber scraper.

• Transfer any remaining Eagle® Brand into a storage container, cover and refrigerate. It will keep about one week.

• Use the remaining milk in recipes, in the ideas on page 29 or add it to coffee and tea.

Visit us at
www.eaglebrand.com
or call 1-888-656-3245
for more dessert ideas.

92

Storing Eagle® Brand

Store unopened cans of Eagle® Brand in a cool, dry place—not near the range. Because it is a natural product, Eagle® Brand may vary in color and consistency from can to can. It will become thicker and more caramel-colored when kept on the shelf for a long time. These changes won't affect its quality, however. (Use it in recipes with peanut butter, butterscotch or chocolate—the rich caramel flavor and color will blend well with these ingredients.)

Unopened Eagle® Brand is safe and wholesome as long as the can seal is intact.

☙ Caramel Treats ❧

For an easy caramel topping or dip, simply heat Eagle® Brand and serve it over ice cream or with assorted cookies or fruit (such as bananas, apples, and/or strawberries). For safety reasons, heating an unopened can is not recommended. Instead, use one of these methods to make the caramel:

• **Oven Method:** Pour 1 can Eagle® Brand into a 9-inch pie plate. Cover with foil; place in a larger shallow pan. Fill the larger pan with hot water. Bake at 425° for 1 hour or until thick and caramel-colored. Beat until smooth.

• **Stovetop Method:** Pour 1 can Eagle® Brand into the top of a double boiler; place over boiling water. Over low heat, simmer 1 to 1½ hours or until thick and caramel-colored, stirring occasionally. Beat until smooth.

• **Microwave Method:** Pour 1 can Eagle® Brand into 2-quart glass measuring cup. Cook on 50% power (medium) 4 minutes, stirring briskly every 2 minutes until smooth. Cook on 30% power (medium-low) 20 to 26 minutes or until very thick and caramel-colored, stirring briskly every 4 minutes during the first 16 minutes and every 2 minutes the last 4 to 10 minutes.

—— **Caution: Never heat an unopened can.** ——

Index

Metric Conversion Charts

Metric Cooking Hints

By making a few conversions, cooks in Australia, Canada, and the United Kingdom can use these recipes with confidence. The charts on this page provide a guide for converting measurements from the U.S. customary system, which is used throughout this book, to the imperial and metric systems. There also is a conversion table for oven temperatures to accommodate the differences in oven calibrations.

Product Differences: Most of the ingredients called for in the recipes in this book are available in English-speaking countries. However, some are known by different names. Here are some common American ingredients and their possible counterparts:

■ Sugar is granulated or castor sugar.
■ Powdered sugar is icing sugar.
■ All-purpose flour is plain household flour or white flour. When self-rising flour is used in place of all-purpose flour in a recipe that calls for leavening, omit the leavening agent (baking soda or baking powder) and salt.
■ Light-colored corn syrup is golden syrup.
■ Cornstarch is cornflour.
■ Baking soda is bicarbonate of soda.
■ Vanilla is vanilla essence.
■ Golden raisins are sultanas.

Volume and Weight: Americans traditionally use cup measures for liquid and solid ingredients. The chart, above right, shows the approximate imperial and metric equivalents. If you are accustomed to weighing solid ingredients, the following approximate equivalents will be helpful.

■ 1 cup butter, castor sugar, or rice = 8 ounces = about 250 grams
■ 1 cup flour = 4 ounces = about 125 grams
■ 1 cup icing sugar = 5 ounces = about 150 grams

Spoon measures are used for smaller amounts of ingredients. Although the size of the tablespoon varies slightly in different countries, for practical purposes andfor recipes in this book, a straight substitution is all that's necessary.

Measurements made using cups or spoons always should be level unless stated otherwise.

Equivalents: U.S. = Australia/U.K.

⅛ teaspoon = 0.5 ml
¼ teaspoon = 1 ml
½ teaspoon = 2 ml
1 teaspoon = 5 ml
1 tablespoon = 1 tablespoon
¼ cup = 2 tablespoons = 2 fluid ounces = 60 ml
⅓ cup = ¼ cup = 3 fluid ounces = 90 ml
½ cup = ⅓ cup = 4 fluid ounces = 120 ml
⅔ cup = ½ cup = 5 fluid ounces = 150 ml
¾ cup = ⅔ cup = 6 fluid ounces = 180 ml
1 cup = ¾ cup = 8 fluid ounces = 240 ml
1¼ cups = 1 cup
2 cups = 1 pint
1 quart = 1 liter
½ inch =1.27 cm
1 inch = 2.54 cm

Baking Pan Sizes

American	Metric
8×1½-inch round baking pan	20×4-cm cake tin
9×1½-inch round baking pan	23×3.5-cm cake tin
11×7×1½-inch baking pan	28×18×4-cm baking tin
13×9×2-inch baking pan	30×20×3-cm baking tin
2-quart rectangular baking dish	30×20×3-cm baking tin
15×10×1-inch baking pan	30×25×2-cm baking tin (Swiss roll tin)
9-inch pie plate	22×4- or 23×4-cm pie plate
7- or 8-inch springform pan	18- or 20-cm springform or loose-bottom cake tin
9×5×3-inch loaf pan	23×13×7-cm or 2-pound narrow loaf tin or pâté tin
1½-quart casserole	1.5-liter casserole
2-quart casserole	2-liter casserole

Oven Temperature Equivalents

Fahrenheit Setting	Celsius Setting*	Gas Setting
300°F	150°C	Gas Mark 2 (slow)
325°F	160°C	Gas Mark 3 (moderately slow)
350°F	180°C	Gas Mark 4 (moderate)
375°F	190°C	Gas Mark 5 (moderately hot)
400°F	200°C	Gas Mark 6 (hot)
425°F	220°C	Gas Mark 7
450°F	230°C	Gas Mark 8 (very hot)
Broil		Grill

*Electric and gas ovens may be calibrated using Celsius. However, for an electric oven, increase the Celsius setting 10 to 20 degrees when cooking above 160°C. For convection or forced-air ovens (gas or electric), lower the temperature setting 10°C when cooking at all heat levels.